Quick Work

A short course in Business English

David Grant
Robert McLarty

OXFORD

1 OUT AND ABOUT *page 4*

SECTION	INPUT TEXT	LANGUAGE WORK	OUTPUT TASK
Introductions	Listening • personal introductions	Present simple	Exchanging personal and professional information
Asking for information	Listening • facilities at an airport	*Is there/Are there?* *Where is?* *What time/When?* Telling the time Prepositions of place	Asking about hotel facilities
Requests	Listening • website addresses • getting through on the telephone	Requests and responses How to say symbols in Internet addresses	Making requests on the telephone
Friendly welcomes	Listening • a company visitor	Offers and responses: *Would you like …?*	Meeting and welcoming a visitor to your company
Describing jobs	Reading • job titles Listening • a company organization chart	Describing responsibilities: *report to, responsible for, in charge of, manage*	Explaining who people are and what they do in your company
Conference talk	Listening • conversations in different situations	Revision	Board game – at a conference

2 PRESENTING YOUR COMPANY *page 16*

Describing companies	Reading and listening • company descriptions	Describing company activities Names of markets	Asking questions about companies
Facts and figures	Listening • facts and figures about SF	*How much/many …?* Saying numbers and using *about*	Presenting key facts and figures about your company
Current activities	Listening • activities in a company's departments	Present continuous for current actions	Describing your current projects
Personal profiles	Reading • a profile of a senior manager	Simple past Saying the year	Exchanging information about your personal history
Systems and processes	Reading • facts about water	Present tense passives Sequencing: *first, then, next*	Describing an administrative or production process
Company overview	Reading and listening • an overview of BASF	Revision	A brief presentation about your company

3 EXCHANGING INFORMATION *page 28*

Telephoning	Listening • a call to a trade fair organizer	Starting and ending a call Asking for repetition and checking understanding	Phoning a company to get more information about their products/services
Working conditions	Reading • survey questionnaire Listening • discussion about working conditions	Possibility and obligation: *have to, don't have to, can* 'Benefits' vocabulary	Finding out details of working for a different company

SECTION	INPUT TEXT	LANGUAGE WORK	OUTPUT TASK
Making comparisons	Reading • comparing places, objects, and people	Comparatives and superlatives	Choosing the best location for a new retail outlet
Product details	Listening • a call to a supplier	Asking about size, dimensions, weight, etc. Shapes and colours	Phoning for information about an exhibition stand
Organizing an event	Reading • a laser entertainment company	Revision	Organizing an event

4 GETTING THINGS DONE   page 36

SECTION	INPUT TEXT	LANGUAGE WORK	OUTPUT TASK
Checking progress	Listening • checking on progress	Present perfect + *yet*	Getting an update of someone's activities
Dealing with complaints	Listening • dealing with unhappy customers	Saying sorry, making excuses, and stating action Using *very, fairly, quite*, etc.	Listening and responding to a customer's problem
Task management	Listening • discussion about a new project	*We need to/should* *Could you?* *Shall I?* Prepositions of time	Organizing a marketing trip
Checking facts	Reading and listening • calling a hotel to check information	Checking and confirming information Saying prices, days of the week, and dates	Checking and confirming facts about a new hotel
Solving a problem	Reading and listening • time management tips • prioritizing tasks	Revision	Organizing your workload

5 PLANNING AHEAD   page 46

SECTION	INPUT TEXT	LANGUAGE WORK	OUTPUT TASK
Making predictions	Reading • discussing the pros and cons of changing to an on-line catalogue	*will* and *won't*	Presenting ideas for saving or making money
Ideas	Reading and listening • how a brewery owner promotes his business	Making and responding to suggestions	Discussing ideas for an advertising campaign for a high-energy sweet
Arrangements	Reading and listening • organizing speakers for a series of seminars	Present continuous for future plans	Arranging a schedule for learning English on the Internet
Future plans	Reading • Aston Martin's production plans	*going to* *plan to* *hope to*	Planning strategy for a national newspaper
Staying in touch	Listening • ending off a day's visit to a company	Thanking, acknowledging, and referring to future contact	Thanking and saying goodbye in different situations
Making choices	Listening and reading • creating more office space	Revision	Finding office space for a sales team

INFORMATION FILES   page 58   **GLOSSARY**   page 77
TAPESCRIPT   page 70

1 Out and about

In this unit you are going to study ways of asking for and giving information. You will:

introduce yourself to new business contacts

find out where things are

make contact by telephone

make and respond to offers

describe the organization of your company

▶ INTRODUCTIONS

1 What's your name? Where are you from? Who do you work for?

2 [1.1] Two people introduce themselves. Complete the information with these words, then listen and check your answers.

| live | I'm from | introduce | an engineer | My |
| I'm | work for | I am | meet | |

Hello. Can I ¹............... myself? ²............... Sylvie Leray. I ³............... Michelin, in Ladoux in France. ⁴............... a research scientist.

Nice to ⁵............... you. ⁶............... name's Pietro Benedetti. ⁷............... Bologna in Italy originally, but now I ⁸............... in Torino. I'm ⁹............... at Fiat.

3 Work with a partner. Introduce yourself to each other.

QUICK CHECK

1 Do you know what nationality these companies are?

| Sony | Levi Strauss & Co. | BBC |
| Fiat | Samsung | Nokia |

2 Where do people speak these languages? Sometimes there is more than one answer.

| French | Portuguese | Spanish |
| Polish | Arabic | Thai |

4 [1.2] Two people are talking in a hotel bar. Listen and complete the information.

Name	Fernanda Inez	Tomas Sammler
Nationality	....	....
Works in	....	....
Company	El Aguila	Bosch
Products	.... for Spanish market	.... for the car industry

Present simple

We use the Present simple to talk in general about our job, our company, everyday life, etc.

*I'm from Portugal and my colleague is from Brazil.
I work in Amsterdam and my boss works in Brussels.
I don't live/He doesn't live in the city.*

To make questions, we normally use *do* and *does*.
*Who do you/we/they work for?
What does he/she/your company do?*

But with the verb *to be* we say:
*What's (What is) your job?
Where are you/they from?*

5 [1.2] Match a–e to 1–5 to make five questions. Then listen again and check your answers.

a	Where do	1	you based?
b	Who do	2	you?
c	Where are	3	you come from?
d	What about	4	your company do?
e	What does	5	you work for?

6 Work with a partner. Use the information in **4**. One of you is Fernanda and the other is Tomas. Ask and answer the questions in **5**.

7 Complete the questions in this conversation then practise it with a partner.

A   Hello. Can I ¹.............. myself? My name's Igor.
B   Oh hello. I'm Karen. ².............. from, Igor?
A   Well, originally I'm from the Ukraine. What ³.............. you?
B   Oh, I'm from Liverpool, but I live in Australia now. ⁴.............. live?
A   I live in Warsaw. I work for a Polish software company. ⁵.............. work for?
B   I work for GlaxoSmithKline.
A   ⁶.............. do?
B   It produces consumer goods, like toothpaste and soft drinks.

Task

1 Write down some questions that you can ask someone you meet for the first time. Write as many questions as you can with these words.

Who …?   What …?   Where …?

2 Introduce yourself to other people in your group. Take it in turns to ask and answer each other's questions. If someone asks one of your questions before you do, say *What about you?* It's not necessary to repeat the question.

ASKING FOR INFORMATION

1 What services and facilities do good international airports have?

2 Match the signs on the airport floor plan below with the names of the facilities in a–h.

e.g. *café/bar* ...*1*...

a left luggage ....
b telephones ....
c lifts ....
d toilets ....
e first-aid room ....
f information desk ....
g car-rental desk ....
h bureau de change ....

3 Look at the plan again. Where do you/can you:

a show your ticket and register your luggage?
b ask about transport to your hotel?
c buy presents to take home?
d change money?
e sometimes need to open your suitcase?
f buy a plane ticket?
g get medical help?

QUICK CHECK

Match the prepositions to the pictures.

on the left   on the right   between   next to
over there   opposite   behind   in front of

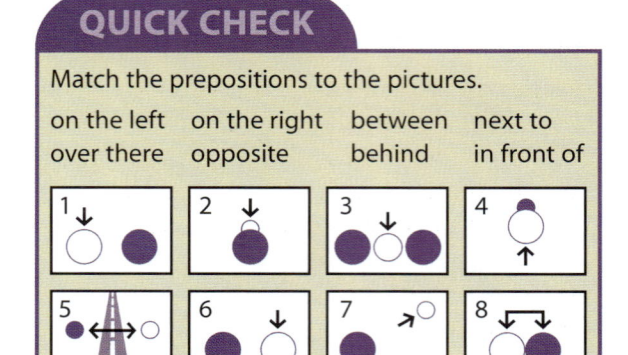

4 [1.3] You are at point A on the plan, the main entrance is behind you. Listen to someone describing the facilities in the airport. What facilities are they talking about?

a ....
b ....
c ....
d ....
e ....

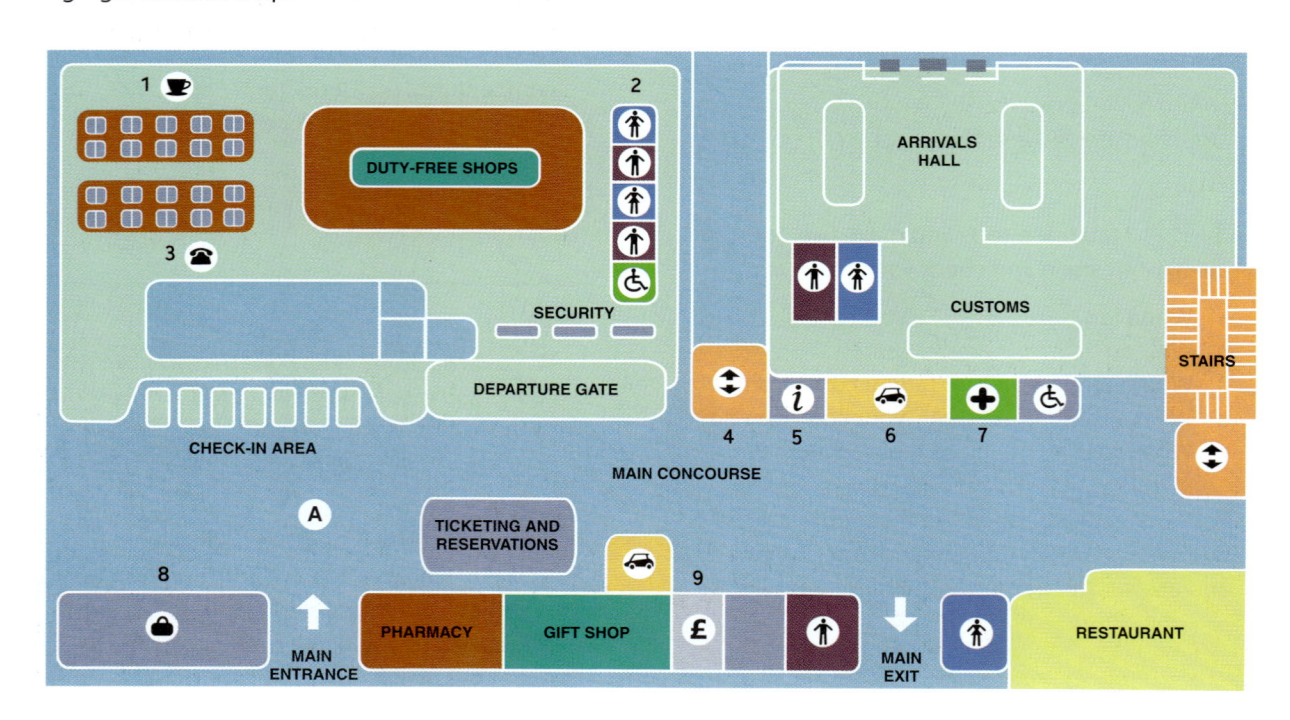

5 🔊1.4 Complete the questions for the answers in **4**. Listen and check your answers.

a Excuse me. Where's *the check-in area*?
b Excuse me. Is ....?
c Excuse me. Where's ....?
d Excuse me. Are ....?
e Excuse me. Where are ....?

6 Work with a partner. Ask and answer the questions in **5**.

Asking about services

We use *Is there …?/Are there …?* to ask if a service or facility exists.

Is there *a bank near here?*
Yes, ***there is. There's*** *one at the end of the road.*
Are there *any trains on a Sunday morning?*
No, ***there aren't.*** *The first one is at 13.30.*

We use *Where is …?/Where are …?* to ask where something is.

Where's *the information desk?*
Where are *the lifts?*

7 Work with a partner. You're at the information desk. Ask and answer questions about other places in the airport.

Is there …?   Are there …?   Where's …?   Where are …?

8 🔊1.5 Look at these signs. Listen to some airport staff giving information to travellers. Write the missing times.

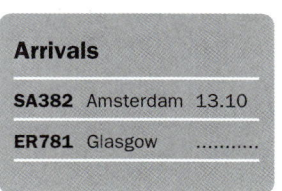

Arrivals

SA382 Amsterdam 13.10
ER781 Glasgow   ....

Departures

AT212 Frankfurt   ....
SO341 Budapest   12.55

Airport Shops

Opening hours
Mon–Sat: 06.30– ....
Sun: 06.30– ....

Bureau de change
Open 7 days
09.00 – ....

9 🔊1.5 Listen again and complete these questions from the first three conversations.

a What time .... the plane from Glasgow ....?
b What time .... the shops .... here?
c What time .... they ....?
d What time .... it ....?

10 Work with a partner. Ask and answer some similar questions about the information in **8**.

Task

Work with a partner. You are a hotel guest and hotel receptionist. One person should use the information in File 4 on page 59 and the other should use the information in File 37 on page 69.

QUICK CHECK

How do you say these times? Think of two ways to say each one.

e.g. 1 *quarter past four* or *four fifteen*

1 16:15
2 (clock showing 4:30)
3  17:10
4 (clock showing 10:45)
5  21:55
6 (clock showing 12:00)

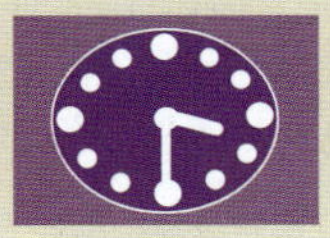

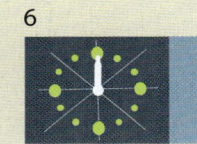

REQUESTS

1 Can you spell your name in English? And your company's name? Can you say your e-mail address and your telephone number in English? What about your company's website address?

QUICK CHECK

Match the symbols with their names.

1	/	a	underscore
2	t_s	b	at
3	t-d	c	dot
4	@	d	dash
5	www.	e	forward slash

2 Look at this advertisement. Work with a partner and decide how to say the telephone number and the two Internet addresses.

smile — the Internet bank from The Co-operative Bank

smile is the UK's first Internet bank, offering a full range of banking services.
For further information, phone
0161 477 1927
or e-mail us at
enquiry@smile.co.uk
For a demonstration of our services, visit
www.smile.co.uk/demo

3 [1.6] Now listen to this radio advertisement and check your answers.

4 Work with a partner. One person should use the information in File 5 on page 59 and the other should use the information in File 21 on page 63.

5 [1.7] Listen to someone making a phone call. Complete the information on his business card.

.... SYSTEMS
121 Godwyn Park, Abingdon, UK

Philip ....
Regional Sales Manager

Tel: 01235 679888
Fax: 01235 679840
Cell phone: ....
e-mail: .... @ ....

6 [1.7] Listen to the conversation again and complete the sentences.

a .... speak to Alex Fielding, please?
b .... ask him to call me back tomorrow?
c .... tell me your name, please?
d .... have your phone number?
e .... take your e-mail address too?

Requests

We say *Can/Could I …?* when we want to do something.

Can I speak to Rebecca West, please?
Could I have a copy of the address list, please?

We use *Can/Could you …?* when we want another person to do something.

Can you give me your number?
Could you repeat that, please?

To respond positively, we can say:

Could you spell your name, please?
Yes, of course./Yes, certainly./Sure.

We use *I'm afraid* to say that something is not possible.

Can I speak to Rebecca West, please?
I'm afraid she's not here today.

7 For each situation, make polite requests using *can/could* and the words in *italics*.

e.g.
Receptionist *Could you sign the register, please?*
Guest *Can I use your pen, please?*

a Receptionist *sign/register?*
   Guest *use/pen?*
b Customer *pay/credit card?*
   Shop assistant *sign/credit card receipt?*
c Tourist *change/traveller's cheques?*
   Bank employee *see/passport?*
d Waiter *take/plate?*
   Customer *bring/bill?*
e Air hostess *fasten/seatbelt?*
   Passenger *use/cell phone?*

8 Think of responses to the requests in **7**. Practise the requests and reponses with a partner.

Receptionist *Could you sign the register, please?*
Guest *Yes, of course. Can I use your pen, please?*
Receptionist *Certainly. Here you are.*

Task

Work with a partner. You are going to have two telephone conversations. One person should use the information below and the other should use the information in File 24 on page 64.

1 Phone WPC and ask to speak to the Marketing Manager. If he/she's not there, ask for the Marketing Manager's name, phone number, and e-mail address. Make a note of the information your partner gives you.

Name: ....
E-mail address: ....
Telephone: ....

2 You work for Mateo SA. Your partner will phone you and ask to speak to the Sales Manager. He is in a meeting. Use this information to answer your partner's questions.

MATEO SA

Tibor Penaloza
Sales Manager

E-mail: sales@mateo.com
Tel: 00 1 3254 7222

FRIENDLY WELCOMES

1 Why do people visit companies? Do you visit other companies? For what reasons? Tell a partner.

2 [1.8] Stefan Tiriac is visiting Elena Michelson for a project meeting. Listen to the first part of their conversation and number a–h in the order you hear them.

a How are you? ....
b I'm free all day. ....
c Nice to see you again. ...1...
d Please come in and have a seat. ....
e I'm sorry I'm late. ....
f I'm afraid Oscar is ill today. ....
g Thank you. ....
h Can I plug in my laptop somewhere? ....

3 [1.8] Listen again and make a note of the responses to each phrase. Work with a partner and practise saying the phrases and responses in **2**.

4 [1.9] Listen to the second part of the conversation. Tick (✓) the things that Elena offers Stefan.

a something to eat ....
b a coffee ....
c a chance to meet some more colleagues ....
d a copy of the sales report ....
e the use of her phone ....
f some notepaper ....

5 [1.9] Listen again and complete the offers.

a Would you like .... before we start?
b Would you like .... the other people on the team?
c Would you like .... my phone?
d Would you like ....
   .... take notes?

6 [1.9] What does Stefan say to respond to the offers? Listen again and check.

Offers

When we want to offer something to somebody, we use *Would you like* (+ noun)? or *Would you like to* (+ verb)?

*Would you like **a drink**?*
*Would you like **to see** the factory first?*

When we respond to an offer, we normally thank the other person.
No, thanks. I'm fine.
Thank you, that's very kind of you.

7 Match the offers a–e with the responses 1–5. Work with a partner and practise saying them.

a Would you like a glass of wine? ....
b Would you like to use the phone? ....
c Would you like to leave a message? ....
d Would you like a copy of the report? ....
e Would you like a hand with that? ....

1 Thank you, that's very kind of you. It is a little heavy.
2 No, thanks. I'll call back later.
3 No, thanks. I'm driving.
4 Yes, please. I can read it on the train.
5 No, thank you. I have my cell phone.

8 Look at the cartoons above. You are visiting a customer to give a presentation of your new products. How can you respond to the things your customer says? Work with a partner and practise the conversations.

9 [1.10] A manager (M) meets her visitor (V) in reception, then goes with him to her office. Put these pairs of sentences in the correct order, from 1–6. The first one has been done. Then listen and check your answers.

☐ M Yes, it is. Please come in.
    V Thank you.
☐ M Have a seat.
    V Thanks very much.
☐ M Right. Here we are.
    V Thank you. Mm, what a lovely office!
☐ M OK, just one second. Here you are.
    V Thanks very much.
[1] M Let's go to my office. It's this way.
    V OK, after you.
☐ M Would you like a coffee?
    V Yes, please. That would be nice.

Task

Work with a partner. One person should use the information below and the other should use the information in File 16 on page 62.

You arrive at your partner's company to present a report. Your partner will meet you, show you to the conference room, and give you any help you need. Before the conversation, decide what to say for each point below. Follow the example. During the conversation, listen carefully to your partner and respond to the things they say.

- Respond to your partner's greeting.
  I'm very well, thanks. And you?
- Say you are sorry that you are a bit late – say why.
- Walk with your host to the conference room. Say something about the building you're in.
- Say something about the conference room – it's nice and big but very hot!
- You only have thirty copies of your report – ask if this is enough.
- Ask if it's possible to use a photocopier.
- Ask if you have time to make a call before you start.

DESCRIBING JOBS

1 What's your job title? How important are job titles in your company or country?

2 Some people are describing their jobs. Read the descriptions and complete their job titles with these words.

Financial   Personal   Area   Chief
Business   Officer   Research Resources

I'm in charge of the sales team in one of our markets.

a .... Sales Manager

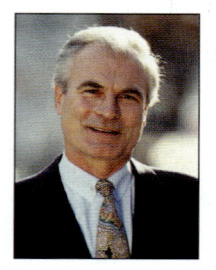

I'm the senior manager of the company.

b .... Executive ....

I'm responsible for finding new markets or products for the company.

c .... Development Manager

I work on the technical design of possible new products.

d .... Engineer

I find new staff and work on employee relations.

e Director of Human ....

I manage the company accounts and other money matters.

f .... Director

I'm the administrator for one of our senior managers – I report to the Marketing Director.

g .... Assistant (PA)

3 Are there people in your company with similar job titles to those in **2**? Give the names of three of them to a partner. Spell them if necessary.

e.g.
Our Area Sales Manager for Western Europe is Marco Schultz. That's S-C-H-U-L-T-Z.

Job responsibilities

To explain a colleague's role in the company, we can say:

*Mr Sukarno **is responsible for** exports.*
*The Personnel Officer is **in charge of** recruiting new staff.*
*Mark **manages** the accounts/a team of five people.*

To explain who a person's boss is, we can say:
*She **reports to** the Marketing Director.*

4 [1.11] The Chief Executive Officer (CEO) of SoftPlan, a computer software company, is explaining the organization of his company to a visitor. Listen and complete the chart.

to **optimize**   to make sure something is as good as possible

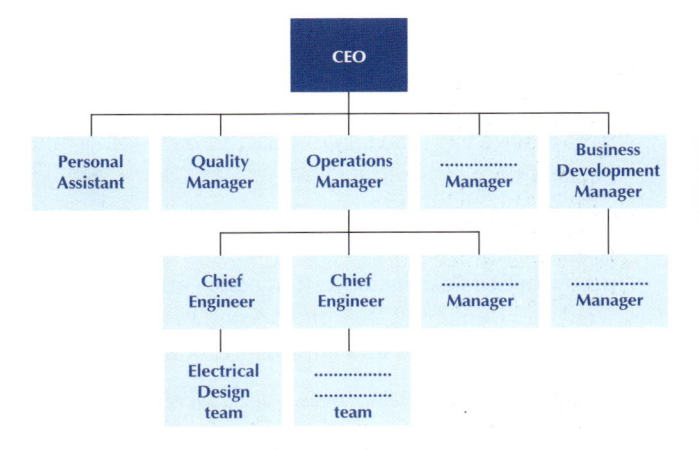

```
                              CEO
         ┌────────┬────────┬────────┬────────┬────────┐
      Personal  Quality  Operations  ......   Business
      Assistant Manager  Manager    Manager   Development
                                              Manager
                           │          │
                    ┌──────┴──┐   ┌───┴───┐
                  Chief     Chief  ......  ......
                  Engineer  Engineer Manager Manager
                    │         │
                Electrical  ......
                Design      team
                team
```

5 Who are Tom Saverys and Petra Mantegazza?

6 Choose a phrase or word from each column in the table below to make complete sentences about the people in the organization chart in **4**.

a	The Production Manager	is responsible for	the Electrical Design and Software Development teams.
b	Four managers	is in charge of	optimizing sales.
c	The Sales Manager	manage	the CEO.
d	The Business Development Manager	reports to	the factory.
e	Two Chief Engineers	manages	finding new markets.
f	The Sales Manager	report to	the Business Development Manager.

7 [1.11] Listen to the conversation again and compare your sentences with those of the two speakers.

8 Work with a partner. You are going to describe a company organization chart. One person should use the information below and the other should use the information in File 20 on page 63.

1 Describe this chart to your partner, who will draw it. You are the Personnel Manager.
   e.g.
   I'm the Personnel Manager. I'm responsible for … I report to …

2 Listen to your partner's description and draw the organization chart.

```
                 Director of Human Resources
                      5 companies in group
         ┌──────────────────┬──────────────────┐
   Personnel Manager                      Personal Assistant
   • finds new staff                      • administrative work
   • team of 10 people
         │
   Training Manager
   • organizes courses
   • team of 5 people
```

Task

Draw an organization chart for your company, or a part of your company. Work with a partner. Explain what each person is responsible for and who they report to.

CONFERENCE TALK

1 [1.12] Listen to four conversations and match them to the pictures a–d.

2 [1.12] Listen to the first conversation again.

a Where's the bank? Is it A, B, C, or D?

b [1.12] What time does the bank open? At 8.45, 9.15, or 9.45?

3 [1.12] Match the first parts of the questions a–e to their endings 1–5. Who is speaking in each case, the customer (C) or the waiter (W)? Listen to the second conversation again and check your answers.

a Could we have
b Can I
c Would you like to
d Would you like
e Could you bring

1 us a bottle of champagne, please?
2 a table next to a window, please?
3 a drink before your meal?
4 take your coats?
5 come this way?

4 [1.12] Listen to the third conversation again and complete the information about Ms Marlet.

Name: Marlet
Comes from: ....
Responsible for: ....
Reports to: ....

5 [1.12] In the fourth conversation you only hear what the caller says. Listen again, and write what you think the other person says in a–e. Work with a partner and compare your answers.

a I'm afraid .... Would .... to his assistant?
b Yes, ... Could I have ...., ...?
c OK, I've .... And could you .... your name, please?
d Right, Mrs Broadbent. I'll give him ....
e You're ....

6 [1.13] Now listen to both sides of the fourth conversation and check your answers. Practise the conversation with a partner.

Task

Play this game with a partner. You are at a drinks party on the first evening of a conference.

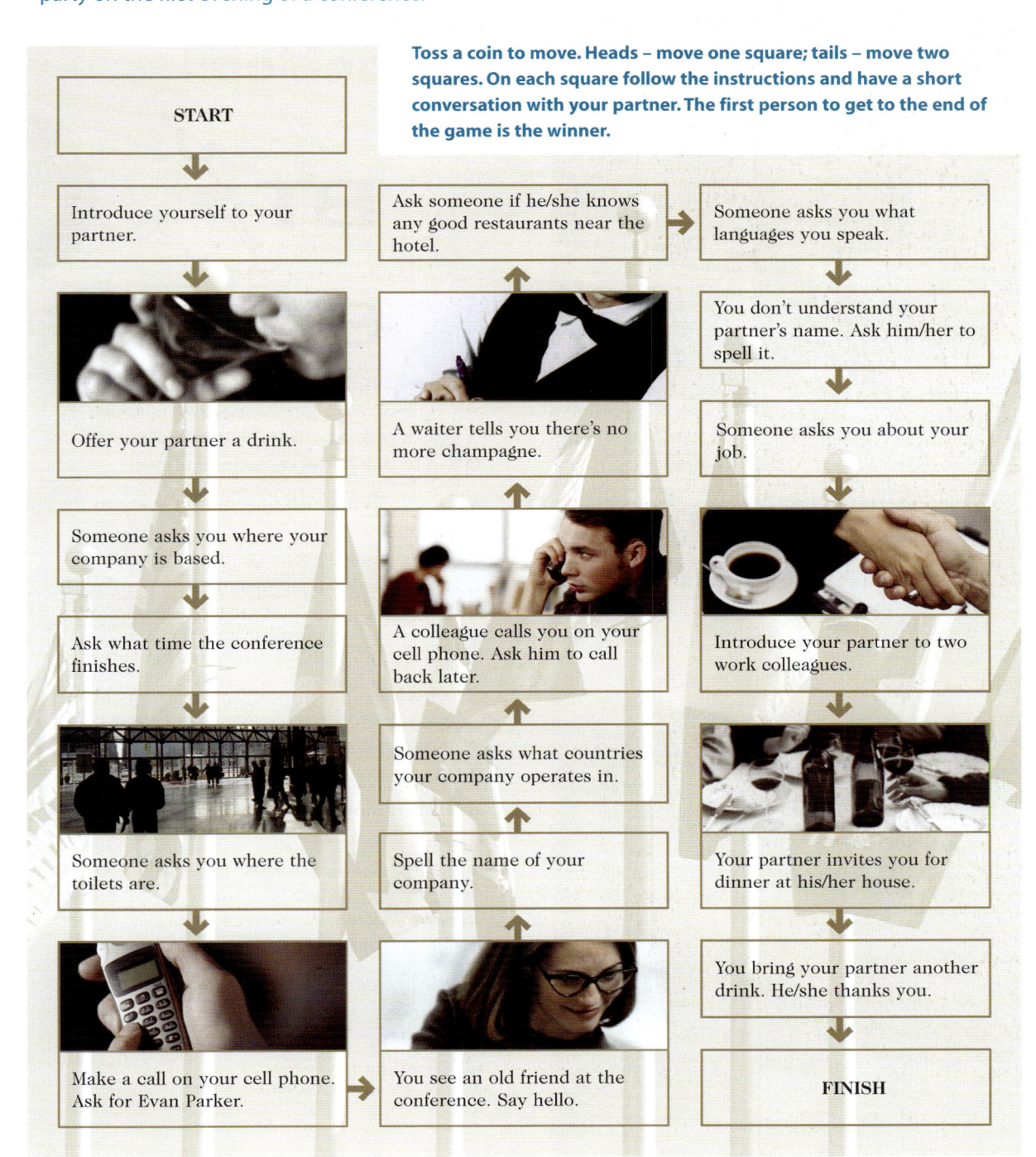

Toss a coin to move. Heads – move one square; tails – move two squares. On each square follow the instructions and have a short conversation with your partner. The first person to get to the end of the game is the winner.

START

↓

Introduce yourself to your partner.

↓

Offer your partner a drink.

↓

Someone asks you where your company is based.

↓

Ask what time the conference finishes.

↓

Someone asks you where the toilets are.

↓

Make a call on your cell phone. Ask for Evan Parker. →

You see an old friend at the conference. Say hello.

↑

Spell the name of your company.

↑

Someone asks what countries your company operates in.

↑

A colleague calls you on your cell phone. Ask him to call back later.

↑

A waiter tells you there's no more champagne.

↑

Ask someone if he/she knows any good restaurants near the hotel. →

Someone asks you what languages you speak.

↓

You don't understand your partner's name. Ask him/her to spell it.

↓

Someone asks you about your job.

↓

Introduce your partner to two work colleagues.

↓

Your partner invites you for dinner at his/her house.

↓

You bring your partner another drink. He/she thanks you.

↓

FINISH

2 Presenting your company

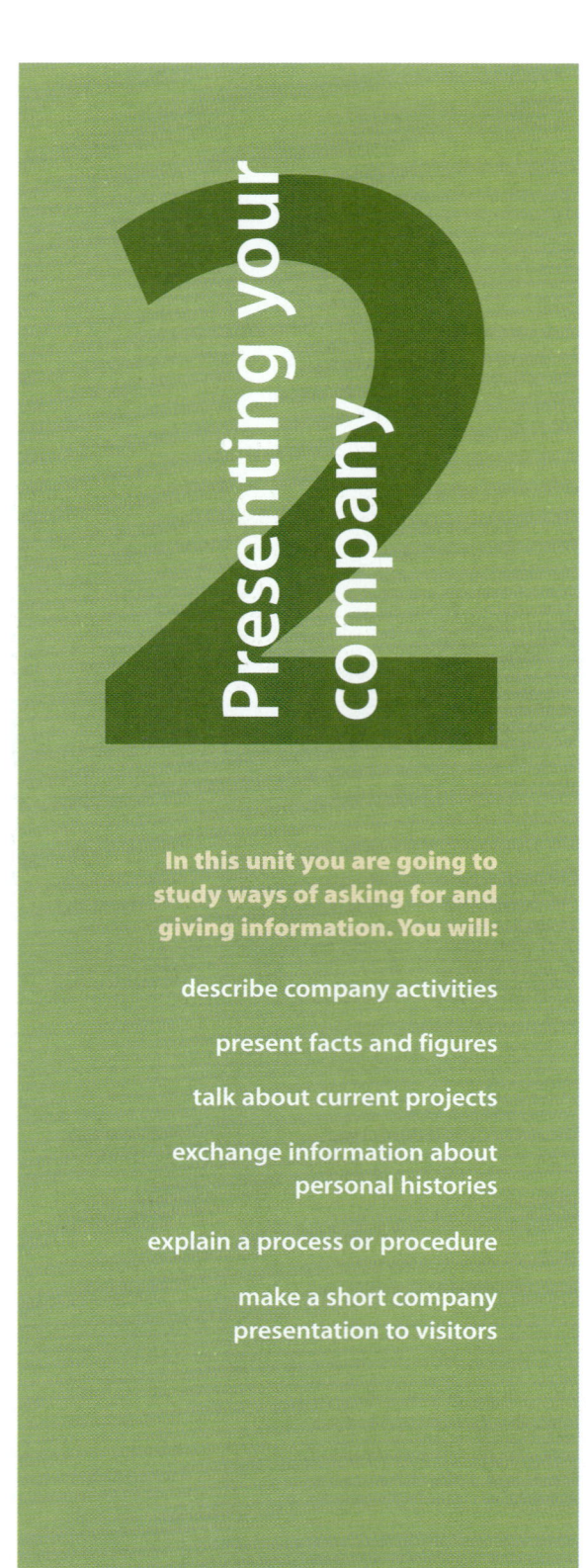

In this unit you are going to study ways of asking for and giving information. You will:

- describe company activities
- present facts and figures
- talk about current projects
- exchange information about personal histories
- explain a process or procedure
- make a short company presentation to visitors

> DESCRIBING COMPANIES

NOKIA Connecting People **IKEA**

ExxonMobil

BT **BMW**

SONY

1 Work with a partner. Match the descriptions in a–e to one of the companies above.

a …………… is a British telecommunications company.
b …………… is a German car manufacturer.
c …………… is a Korean electronics manufacturer.
d …………… is a multinational food company.
e …………… is a Swedish furniture retailer.

2 Now take it in turns to make sentences about the other companies above. Your partner must guess the name of the company. Use these words to help you. You can use some of the words more than once.

Japanese	pharmaceutical	international	European
Asian	telecommunications	clothing	oil
electronics	manufacturer	car	Finnish
producer	plane	Swiss	Italian
retailer	company		

A *It's an Italian clothing manufacturer and retailer.*
B *Benetton?*
A *That's right.*

NOVARTIS

AIRBUS

mazda

Nestlé

SAMSUNG ELECTRONICS

UNITED COLORS OF BENETTON.

3 [2.1] Work with a partner and say what these companies do. Then listen and check your answers.

a	McDonald's	operates	*Time* and *Fortune* magazines.
b	General Motors	publishes	cars and other vehicles.
c	Thomas Cook Travel	constructs	cell phone networks.
d	Cellnet	sells	software solutions.
e	Sekisui House	manufactures	package holidays.
f	Banco Bradesco	organizes	fast food all over the world.
g	AOL Time Warner	provides	luxury homes.
h	IBM	produces	banking services.

to construct to build
luxury expensive and high quality
networks systems that are linked together
package holiday a holiday at a fixed price which includes travel, hotel, etc.
to publish to print and distribute to the public
software programmes for computers

4 Now take it in turns to ask your partner what the companies in **1** and **2** do. If you don't know say: *I don't know. Do you?*

A *What does IKEA do?*
B *It sells furniture.*

5 [2.2] Listen to managers from three of the companies in **3**. Complete the table below, then decide with a partner which company it is.

Company name	Main activities	Other activities
1	.... houses, restaurants, and ....; manages big	.... and information systems
2	....	.... trucks
3	provides a range of .... and .... services	.... insurance; offers free .... to customers

6 Work with a partner and ask and answer questions about the three companies.

e.g.
Where does the company operate?
What does it produce/provide/sell?
What other activities does it have?

Task

1 Work with a partner. Think of five well-known companies but don't tell your partner the names. Take it in turns to ask each other questions to find out what the companies are. First make a list of the questions you can ask.

e.g.
Where is the company based? Is it an American company?

2 Now ask your partner similar questions about their own company.

FACTS AND FIGURES

1 What is the population of your country? And your town? What is a good salary in your country?

QUICK CHECK

1 Write these numbers in figures, as in the example.
   a Twenty-six ....*26*....
   b Seven hundred and fifty ....
   c One thousand five hundred ....
   d Ten thousand ....
   e Eighty-nine thousand ....
   f Four hundred and fifty thousand ....
   g One and a half million ....

2 How do you say these numbers?
   89   627   52,500   2,320

3 When we don't know the exact number or it's not important, we usually say *about* (+ number). So, for 98 or 102, we can say: *about a hundred*. Now say the numbers in 2 again using *about*.

2 [2.3] Listen to an interview with an engineer from the company SF. Choose the correct answer in *italics* below.

a The company *manufactures planes/supplies plane parts/constructs airports*.
b It's head office is in *Eindhoven/Essen/Emmen*.
c It's a *Dutch/German/Swiss* company.

3 [2.4] Listen to the rest of the interview. Match the numbers a–e with the things they refer to 1–5.

a 1,600   1 office space in m^2
b 19,000   2 number of sites
c 77,000   3 number of employees
d 7   4 annual turnover
e 400,000,000   5 factory space in m^2

annual every year
sites places where a company has factories/offices, etc.
space area occupied by offices/factories, etc.
turnover the value of a company's sales in dollars/pounds, etc.

4 [2.3] [2.4] Complete the questions the interviewer asks. Listen to the whole interview again and check your answers.

a .... does SF do?
b .... are you based?
c .... people do you employ?
d .... are your main customers?
e .... sites do you have?
f .... office space do you have?
g .... money does SF make per year?

5 Work with a partner and ask and answer the questions in **4**.

How many …? How much …?

We use *How many …?* with things that we can count. These words have plural forms.

How many factories are there?
There ***is one*** factory/***are three*** factories.

We use *How much …?* with words that have no plural form.

How much equipment do you have?
We have ***a lot of*** equipment.

Notice we can't say *equipments*.

6 Do we use *How many …?* or *How much …?* with these words?

| cars | wine | hours | computers | phones |
| money | experience | customers | time | |

7 Write three questions to ask your partner with *How much …?* or *How many …?* Use the words in **6** for ideas, then ask your questions.

e.g.
How many customers does your company have?
How much time do you spend learning English?

8 Work with a partner. One person should use the information below and the other should use the information in File 11 on page 61.

Use the information in column A to answer your partner's questions. Then ask your partner questions about the company in column B and complete the table.

QUICK CHECK

1. International companies often divide the world into different markets. With a partner, think of two or three countries in each of these markets.

   e.g. *The Far East: Japan and China*

Western Europe	Eastern Europe
The Middle East	The Far East
North America	South-East Asia
South America	

2. We talk about the Western Europ***ean*** market. How would you describe the other markets?

Task

1 Prepare a short presentation of your company. Include information about:

– its activity
– the number of employees
– where the head office is
– where the offices and/or factories are
– how much office/factory space you have
– your annual turnover
– two or three other interesting facts or figures.

2 Work with a partner. Give your presentation and be ready to answer questions.

3 Listen to your partner's presentation and ask any questions you have.

	A	B
Name of company	Cogema	……………
Activity	produces nuclear power	manufactures ……………
Turnover	about 200 billion euros	about £ ……………
Number of employees	19,000	……………
Sites	operates 59 nuclear reactors and 5 uranium production sites in France	head office in …………… and factory in ……………
Interesting fact	nuclear power provides 80% of France's electricity	exports ……………% of its products

CURRENT ACTIVITIES

1 Look at the cartoon and match these names of different departments to a–f.

Finance IT
Sales & Marketing Human Resources
Research & Development Front office/Reception

2 Which department:

a provides computer support?
b produces sales reports?
c develops new products?
d does the accounts?
e recruits staff?
f deals with visitors?

What other departments do you find in companies? What do they do?

3 [2.5] Listen to the receptionist calling three departments to ask for help. Do they offer to help her? Why/Why not?

4 [2.5] Listen again. Tick (✓) the excuses she hears. Which departments gave these excuses?

a I'm interviewing candidates. ....
b We're doing our monthly figures. ....
c I'm checking the phones. ....
d We're preparing a new advertising campaign. ....
e We're doing tests on a new product. ....

Present continuous

We use the Present continuous to describe actions happening around *now*.

She can't come at the moment because she's (she is) talking to a customer.
What are you doing at the moment?
Are you working today?   Yes, I am./No, I'm not.
We're (We are) working on three new projects this year.

5 Look at the cartoon above again. Describe what is happening in each office.

6 [2.6] Complete this conversation with the correct form of the words in brackets. Then listen and check your answers.

A So why ¹............... (you travel) round Spain?
B ²............... (We develop) a new product for the Spanish market, so ³............... (I visit) customers here to find out what they want. What about you? What ⁴............... (you do) here?
A ⁵............... (We work) on a project with a Spanish company. ⁶............... (We look) at ways to promote business travel in this area. Where ⁷............... (you stay)?
B At the Hilton. And you?
A Oh, ⁸............... (I stay) with some friends who live in Bilbao.

7 What are people doing at JOB today? Work with a partner. One of you should use the information below and the other should use the information in File 22 on page 64.

Ask your partner questions to find out the missing information and answer your partner's questions.

e.g. *Who is Björn interviewing?*

Task

1 What are you working on at the moment? And what's happening in your department or in your company? Make notes in the table below about your current projects. It's not necessary to write something in every box.

	This year	This month	Today
Me	learning English		
My department			a customer is visiting us
My company			

2 Now tell your partner about your present projects. Give as many details as possible. Then, listen to your partner's description and ask for more details.

A *We're working on a project with a French company.*
B *What are you doing?*
A *We're building a new factory in Lille.*

JOHNSON, OLSON & BRONSON

Staff schedule for today
Tuesday, 7 July

HUMAN RESOURCES
Angela – training new secretaries
Björn – interviewing ....

SALES AND MARKETING
Peter – making a presentation to European sales reps
Valerie – ....

FINANCE
Angus – finishing .... (no interruptions please)
Melissa – preparing the budget

IT
Patrick – developing new software for Finance Department
Sophia – meeting ....

R & D
Maria – testing of ....
Thomas – not working today

FRONT OFFICE
Sarah – welcoming Japanese visitors
William – ....

PERSONAL PROFILES

1 When did you join your present company? Where did you work before and when did you join?

QUICK CHECK

1 Write the year in figures:
   a nineteen eighty-five ....
   b eighteen oh three ....
   c two thousand and one ....
   d two thousand and fifteen ....

2 Say these years:
   1901   1945   1968   1999   2001   2010

2 Read the text below about Kevin Gaskell and complete the text with these verbs.

climbed	became	stayed	celebrated
won	joined	moved	left
enjoyed	*studied*	got	

3 Work with a partner and ask and answer these questions about the text.

a What did he do at university?
b What happened in 1981?
c What happened in 1982?
d What did he do in 1996?
e Where did he go in 2000?
f How did he celebrate his fortieth birthday?

Talking about the past

To talk about past events we normally use the Simple past.

Regular verbs end in *-ed*.
Yesterday she finish**ed** work at 8 o'clock.
He start**ed** working for the company in 1998.

Irregular verbs have many different forms. Some common ones are:

go – *went*   have – *had*
do – *did*   come – *came*

We use *did* to make past questions.
What **did** he **study**? He studi**ed** science.
Where **did** they **go** last week? They **went** to Rome.

When a regular verb ends with a /t/ or /d/ sound, we pronounce the *-ed* ending as /ɪd/.
start**ed**   decid**ed**

Kevin Gaskell is in his early forties and is already in his third senior management position in three different companies! He is the Managing Director of CarsDirect.com, an Internet company which specializes in selling cars. At university he [1] ...*studied*... engineering. In fact, in 1981 he [2] .... the prize for the best engineering student in the whole country. He [3] .... his first job at Porsche UK in 1982. In 1992 he [4] .... Managing Director of the company and [5] .... in that job for four years. He [6] .... the company in 1996 and [7] .... BMW UK. He [8] .... this position a lot but in 2000 he [9] .... to CarsDirect.com. In 1999 he [10] .... his fortieth birthday in an interesting way – he [11] .... Mt Everest!

4 Look again at the verbs in **2**. Which verbs are regular and which are irregular?

5 Make questions for these answers.

a What *did he study at university*?
He studied engineering.
b What ....?
He won a prize for the best student.
c When ....?
He became MD in 1992.
d How long ....?
He stayed there for four years.
e Where ....?
He moved to CarsDirect.com.
f Why ....?
To celebrate his fortieth birthday.

6 What do you know about the two business people in the photos? Which person:

a created a shipping firm?
b founded a clothing company?
c was born in Belgium?
d was born in Turkey?
e married a Kennedy?
f studied art in Europe?

Liz Claiborne

Aristotle Onassis

Now go on to **7** and **8** to see if you were correct.

7 [2.7] Listen and complete the information about Aristotle Onassis.

Year	
1906	Born in Turkey
1923	.... to Argentina / .... for a telephone company
1946	.... first oil tanker
1953	.... Olympic Maritime in Monte Carlo
1963	.... Greek island Scorpios
1968	....
1975	Died

8 Work with a partner. You are going to find out about Liz Claiborne's life. One of you should use the information in File 12 on page 61 and the other should use the information in File 15 on page 62.

Task

1 You are going to interview your partner about his/her personal history. Prepare questions to ask about his/her:

– place of birth
– studies
– first job/company
– other jobs/companies
– present job, etc.

2 Ask your questions and make notes of your partner's answers.

3 Tell the rest of the class about three key dates in your partner's career.

e.g.
In 1986 he got his first job with a computer firm.

SYSTEMS AND PROCESSES

1 How much do you know about water? Work with a partner and decide if these sentences are true (T) or false (F). Then check your answers in File 10 on page 60.

True or false?

1 About 51% of the earth is covered by water. ....
2 65% of our body is made of water. ....
3 If the water in our body is reduced by 10%, we will die. ....
4 Bottled water contains no chlorine. Sometimes it is disinfected with ozone. ....
5 Most bottled water is taken from underground springs. ....
6 More bottled water is drunk in the USA than soft drinks. ....

to **disinfect** to clean/purify
to **reduce** to make smaller/less

soft drinks non-alcoholic drinks, like cola
a **spring** a natural source of water

The passive

We often use the passive form of the verb when the person doing the action is unknown or not important. It is formed with the verb *to be* + past participle.

Water **is extracted** from underground springs.
The goods **are delivered** three times a week.
The products **are sold** in supermarkets.

For all regular verbs and many irregular verbs the past participle is the same as the Simple past form. Here are some common *irregular* forms.

Verb	Simple past	Past participle
sell	sold	sold
buy	bought	bought
make	made	made
take	took	taken
give	gave	given

2 Complete the sentences below using the passive form of one of these verbs.

make   check   deliver   use
transport   sell   label   pack

a   The mail .... twice a day.
b   Goods .... by road, rail, sea, or air.
c   This product .... in China but .... in shops in Europe and the US.
d   These rooms .... for management meetings.
e   Glass bottles .... carefully and the package .... 'fragile'.
f   The machine .... for faults every two days.

3 [2.8] Listen to someone describing a product. What is it?

4 Which verbs below did the speaker use? Can you remember what he said?

e.g. sell: It's sold in restaurants and supermarkets.

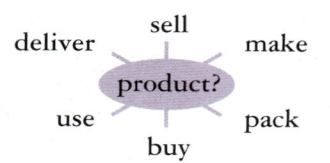

deliver   sell   make
product?
use   pack
buy

[2.8] Listen again and check your answers.

5 Write a similar description of another product, using the passive form. Read it to your partner, who must guess what it is. Use the words in **4** for ideas.

6 [2.9] Listen to a manager of an American water company describing how bottled water is produced. Put the pictures in the correct order 1–8.

7 [2.9] Listen again and complete these notes.

The water is:

a .... from the spring.
b .... to the plant by special trucks.
c filtered to .... sand.
d .... to remove bacteria.
e .... in laboratories for purity.
f ....

The bottles are:

g ....
h .... to the stores.

QUICK CHECK

Use *then*, *finally*, *first*, *next* to complete this description of buying something on the Internet.

a .... the products are selected.
b .... the total price is shown.
c .... the customer's credit card or account number is taken.
d .... the products are sent out to the customer.

8 Work with a partner. Use *first*, *then*, etc. to describe the stages of the process in **6**. Look at the pictures in **6** but cover your notes in **7**.

Task

Prepare a short talk with pictures/diagrams of a process you know well. Here are some ideas and some useful verbs you could use.

PROCESS	USEFUL VERBS
how a product is made	buy/manufacture/assemble/test/pack
how new staff are recruited	advertise/select/interview/send/offer
how a letter arrives at its destination	post/transport/sort/deliver/fly

COMPANY OVERVIEW

1 Look at the information about BASF and choose the correct heading for each fact file a–d.

Products   Key figures   Key dates   Present projects

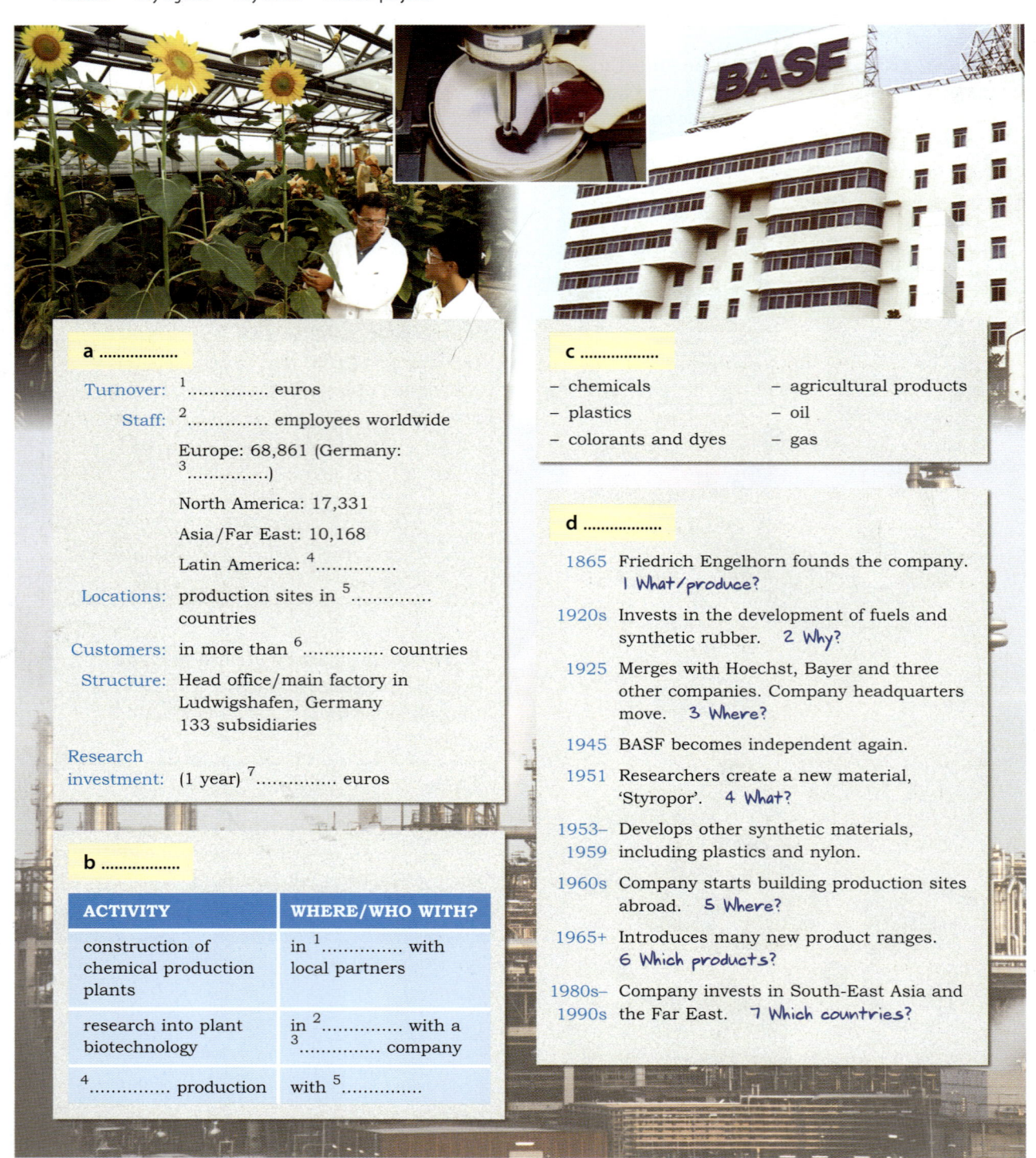

a ....

Turnover: ^{1}............... euros

Staff: ^{2}............... employees worldwide

Europe: 68,861 (Germany: ^{3}...............)

North America: 17,331

Asia/Far East: 10,168

Latin America: ^{4}...............

Locations: production sites in ^{5}............... countries

Customers: in more than ^{6}............... countries

Structure: Head office/main factory in Ludwigshafen, Germany
133 subsidiaries

Research investment: (1 year) ^{7}............... euros

b ....

ACTIVITY	WHERE/WHO WITH?
construction of chemical production plants	in ^{1}............... with local partners
research into plant biotechnology	in ^{2}............... with a ^{3}............... company
^{4}............... production	with ^{5}...............

c ....

– chemicals
– plastics
– colorants and dyes
– agricultural products
– oil
– gas

d ....

1865   Friedrich Engelhorn founds the company. *1 What/produce?*

1920s Invests in the development of fuels and synthetic rubber. *2 Why?*

1925   Merges with Hoechst, Bayer and three other companies. Company headquarters move. *3 Where?*

1945   BASF becomes independent again.

1951   Researchers create a new material, 'Styropor'. *4 What?*

1953–1959   Develops other synthetic materials, including plastics and nylon.

1960s Company starts building production sites abroad. *5 Where?*

1965+ Introduces many new product ranges. *6 Which products?*

1980s–1990s   Company invests in South-East Asia and the Far East. *7 Which countries?*

dye a product that changes the colour of a material
key figures important numbers
to **merge** to join (with another company or other companies)
rubber material used to make tyres
a **subsidiary** a company that is part of a bigger organization
synthetic made by combining different substances

2 Look at the *Key figures* fact file.

a **2.10** Work with a partner and fill in these missing numbers. Then listen and check your answers.

170	35.9 bn	100,000	1.5 bn
54,356	38	6,913	

b Now ask and answer questions about the key figures with *How many …?*

A *How many subsidiaries does the company have?*
B *It has 133.*

3 Look at the *Products* fact file. Make one passive sentence for each of the products mentioned, taking a verb from A and a phrase from B below.

e.g. *Oil is refined to make petrol for cars.*

A	B
refine	in the same places as oil
sell	to conserve natural resources
recycle	to make petrol for cars
produce/test	to give colour to textiles
use	to farmers
find	in laboratories

4 Look at the *Present projects* fact file.

a **2.11** Listen and complete the missing information.

b Work with a partner. Have conversations about the different projects.

A *What are they constructing?*
B *They're building chemical production plants.*
A *Where are they building them?*, etc.

5 Look at the *Key dates* fact file.

a With a partner, take it in turns to describe the key dates in BASF's history. Make sure you change all the verbs to the Simple past.

e.g.
Friedrich Engelhorn founded the company in 1865. Then in the 1920s …

b You would like more information about BASF's history. You have made a note of questions to ask. With a partner, say what the complete question is.

e.g.
1 *What did the company produce in 1865?*

c **2.12** Turn to File 3 on page 58 and match the answers to the questions. Then listen and check your answers.

d Practise asking and answering the questions with a partner. Try to answer without looking at File 3.

Task

1 Prepare a short presentation about your company, then give your talk to your partner who is visiting the company for the first time. In your presentation you should mention:

– key figures (turnover, employees, locations, etc.)
– products/services (what they are, where they are produced/sold, etc.)
– two or three present projects (what the company is doing at the moment)
– five or six key dates in the company's history.

2 When you listen to your partner's presentation, be ready to ask questions to get more information.

3 Exchanging information

In this unit you are going to study ways of exchanging information. You will:

make a telephone call to find out information

share information about working conditions

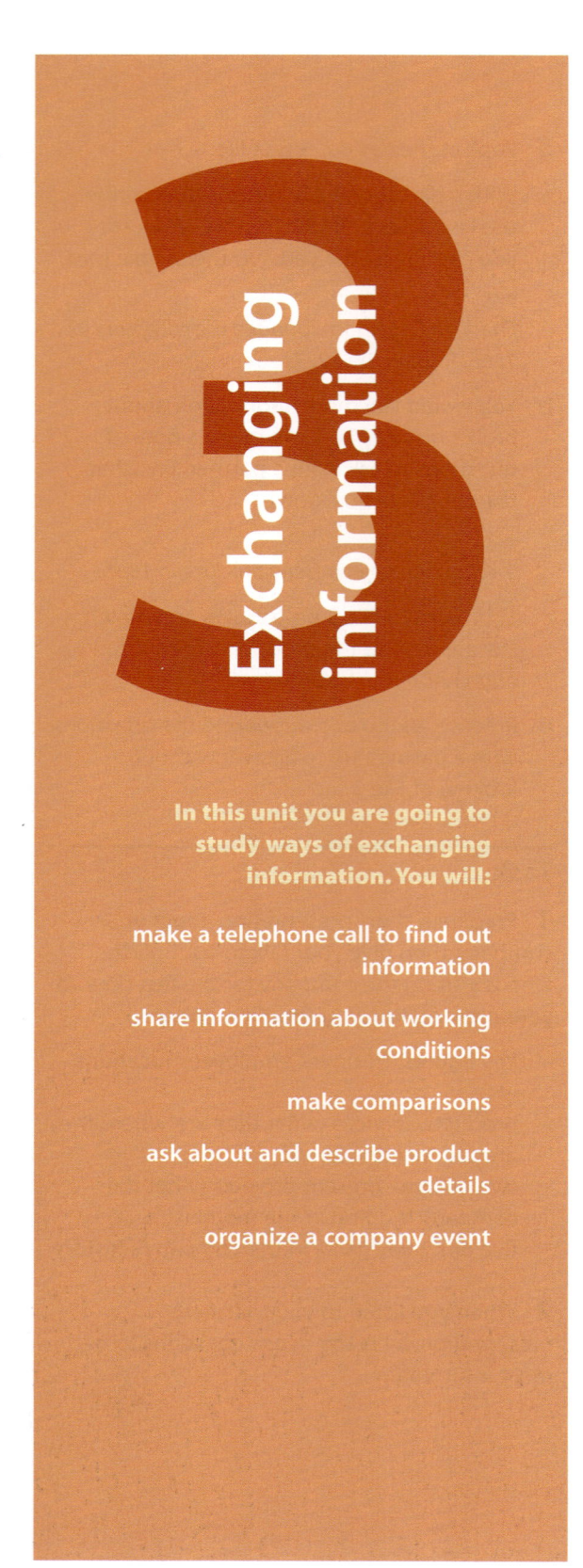

make comparisons

ask about and describe product details

organize a company event

> TELEPHONING

1 How do you introduce yourself on the telephone when you make a call? What do you say when you answer the telephone? How do you end a call?

2 [3.1] Listen to the start of this conversation and answer these questions.

a Is Alan or Danilo making the call?
b Why is he calling?
c What does Veronafiere do?
d How do Alan and Danilo introduce themselves?
e How does Alan ask for information?

3 Work with a partner. One person should look at the information in File 14 on page 62 and the other should look at the information in File 38 on page 69.

4 [3.2] Listen to the rest of the conversation and complete Alan's notes.

> Call Veronafiere – 0039 345 8359621
>
> Is there a fair for the drinks market?
>
> Dates?
>
> Number of visitors to fairs?
>
> Website?

5 [3.2] During the conversation Alan checks the information. Fill in the missing words, then listen again and check your answers.

a Sorry. .... that again, please?
b Sorry, did .... fifty thousand?
c What .... the dates ....?
d Sorry, was .... dot net .... dot I-T?

Making a call

When we start a call, we can say:

This is …
I'm calling from … about …
Could you give me some information, please?

To ask for repetition and to check information, we can say:

Sorry. Was that …
Could you say that again, please?
Sorry, did you say …?

To end the conversation we can say:

Thanks for your help.
Nice talking to you.
Thanks for calling.

6 Match a sentence a–h with a response 1–8.

a Hello, this is Christine Penel.
b My number is 01655 24 …
c Sorry. What was your name?
d Could you send me a brochure, please?
e Did you say J?
f Thank you for your help.
g I'd like some information, please.
h Could you spell that, please?

1 Certainly. What would you like to know?
2 You're welcome. Thanks for calling.
3 No, I said *G* as in *golf*.
4 Certainly. It's P-E-N-E-L.
5 Hello. How can I help you?
6 Christine Penel.
7 Sorry. Was that *double* five?
8 Of course. Can I take your address?

7 Work with a partner. Follow the instructions below. One person receives the call (*A*) and the other person makes the call (*B*).

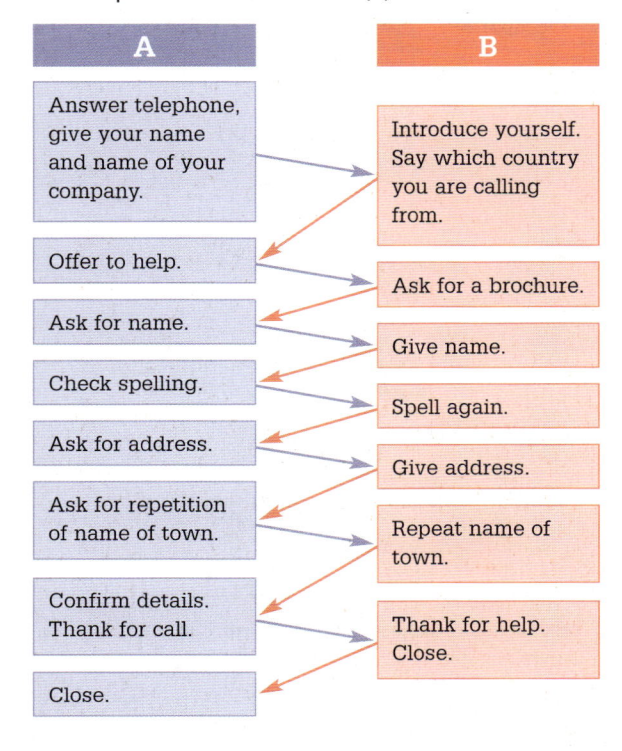

A	B
Answer telephone, give your name and name of your company.	Introduce yourself. Say which country you are calling from.
Offer to help.	Ask for a brochure.
Ask for name.	Give name.
Check spelling.	Spell again.
Ask for address.	Give address.
Ask for repetition of name of town.	Repeat name of town.
Confirm details. Thank for call.	Thank for help. Close.
Close.	

Task

Work with a partner. Look at this advertisement. You are going to find out more information about this organization. One person should look at File 18 on page 63 and the other should look at File 34 on page 67.

JOIN ITC TODAY!

For the best deals on
– flights
– travel insurance
– car rental
– hotels
… and much more. Call us now for details.

ITC International Travellers' Club
Tel: UK (44) London (20) 8256 5525
www.goitc.com

WORKING CONDITIONS

Please take a few minutes to answer the questions below and return the completed form to us.

Occupation: _____ Country: _____

Hours
- How many hours per week do you have to work?
- Do you have to work at weekends?
- Can you choose what time you start/finish work?

Holiday
- How many weeks' holiday do you have?
- Can you take your holiday when you want?
- How many days can you take at a time?

Clothing
- Do you have to wear special clothing like a hard hat, uniform, etc.?
- Can you wear casual clothes to work?

---

casual clothes like jeans and T-shirts, not suits

uniform special clothes that everyone in a company/team wears

1 Look at the questionnaire above and complete it. Discuss your answers with a partner.

2 [3.3] Listen to this conversation and make notes in the table below.

	Karl	Claudia
Hours	short day	long hours
Travel time		
Lunch		
Work late?		
Choose hours of work?		
Holiday		

Possibility and obligation

For things which are necessary we use *have to*.
She **has to** do a report every week.
Do I **have to** write this report?

For things which aren't necessary we use *don't have to*.
I **don't have to** work at night.

For things which are possible we use *can*.
I **can** take language lessons at my company.
Can you take holiday in August?

For things which are not possible we use *can't*.
I **can't** use my cell phone for personal calls.

3 Work with a partner. Ask each other questions about Karl and Claudia. Use the information in the table in **2**.

e.g.
Does Karl have to work late? No he doesn't.
Can Claudia take holidays in July? No, she can't.

QUICK CHECK

Match these words to the definitions below.

health insurance	overtime	company car
pension plan	salary	perks
bonus	training	

a The money you receive each month from your employer.
b Extra benefits, like discounts on company products, free use of sports club, etc.
c Private transport paid for by your employer.
d The money you save for your retirement.
e Lessons and courses where you learn how to do something, e.g. speak English.
f Extra money for working extra hours.
g A plan to pay medical bills.
h Extra money paid for good results/work.

TASK

1 You are going to spend a week working at your partner's company. Prepare a list of ten questions to ask your partner about working conditions in their company. You could ask about:

- working hours
- dress
- language
- lunch
- working late
- personal phone calls
- overtime
- computer use.

2 Now take it in turns to ask each other your questions. If you work for the same company, talk about another company you know well.

4 Look at these two job descriptions. Read them carefully then answer these questions.

a What does Catherine have to do every month?
b Can Jacqueline use her cell phone for personal calls?
c Does Catherine have to work at weekends?
d When does Jacqueline have to report to head office?
e Can Catherine earn overtime?

Make two or three more questions and ask your partner.

Name • Catherine Mercier
Job title • Area Sales Manager
Main activities • Promote a range of office furniture
Benefits • Cell phone
• Company car
• Pension plan
Hours • Up to 45 hours per week, no weekends
• No overtime
Administrative tasks • Organize marketing plan
• Monthly report to Sales Director
Holiday • 6 weeks per year
• Two weeks maximum at one time

Name • Jacqueline Simmons
Job title • Hotel Assistant Manager
Main activities • Organize reception
• Sell conference facilities
Benefits • 50% rates in other hotels in group
• Cell phone – not for personal calls
• Health insurance
Hours • 5 days a week, 3 weekends per month
• 38–41 hours per week – overtime paid
Administrative tasks • Weekly report to head office
Holidays • 5 weeks per year, not to be taken in July or August

MAKING COMPARISONS

1 Look at these photographs.

a Find groups of three things – three film stars (Kate Beckinsale, Meryl Streep, Julia Roberts), three buildings, etc.

b Decide which of these adjectives we can use to describe the items in these groups. For example, we can use *rich* to talk about the film stars.

light	small	healthy	fast	old
rich	expensive	heavy	young	good

2 Decide if these sentences are true (T) or false (F).

a The Leaning Tower of Pisa is older than the CN Tower. ....
b A palmtop computer is lighter than a laptop computer. ....
c The 747 is faster than the Concorde. ....
d Beer is more expensive than champagne. ....
e Meryl Streep is younger than Julia Roberts. ....

Comparatives

When we compare two things we add *-er* to short adjectives (*tall, light, long*, etc.) or use *more* in front of long adjectives (*comfortable, efficient, difficult*, etc.) + *than*.

The River Nile is long**er than** the River Thames.
A Ferrari is **more** expensive **than** a KA.

Adjectives ending in *-y* change to *-ier*.
This exercise is eas**ier than** that exercise.

For *good* and *bad* we use *better* and *worse*.
I think Italian food is **better than** Chinese food.
The weather in Britain is **worse than** in Tahiti.

3 Work with a partner. Look at the pictures above again and make some true and false comparisons like those in **2**. Respond to your partner's statements.

A *Champagne is cheaper than beer.*
B *No it isn't, it's more expensive.*

4 Match the first parts of each sentence a–h with the second parts 1–8.

a China has the longest
b The Eiffel Tower was the highest
c Harvard is one of the best
d James is the commonest
e Larry Ellison is one of the richest
f English is the most important
g Rotterdam is the largest
h Chicago has the busiest

1 first name for a male in the US.
2 business schools in the US.
3 business language.
4 school year with 251 days.
5 port in the world.
6 airport in the world.
7 building constructed in the 19th century.
8 businessmen in the world.

Superlatives

When we compare something to other things in the same group, we add *the* + *-est* to short adjectives, and use *the most* in front of long adjectives. For *good* and *bad* we use *the best* and *the worst*.

*Concorde is **the fastest/best/most expensive** aeroplane in the world.*

5 Complete this table. Add an example sentence for the word which is missing.

Adjective	Comparative	Superlative	Sentence
good	better	the best	French wine is the best.
bad		the worst	
hot	hotter		
wealthy	wealthier		
comfortable	more comfortable		

6 Look at the pictures in **1** and make five questions with superlatives. Work with a partner and ask and answer the questions.

e.g.
Which is the most expensive drink?

7 [3.4] Listen to Tom and Sally comparing lifestyle in three different cities. Where do they work? Where did Tom work before?

8 [3.4] Listen again. What do they say about:

a salaries in New York?
b rent and food in London?
c food in New York?
d amount of tax and length of holidays in each city?

Task

You work for an American clothing company selling T-shirts, sweatshirts, belts, and jeans. You have a factory in Belgium. You want to open your first store in Europe.

1 What factors are important when choosing the location? Work with a partner and make a list.

2 With your partner look at the information in File 2 on page 58. Discuss the three possible locations and decide which one is the best.

3 Present your decision to the class and give reasons for your choice.

PRODUCT DETAILS

1
2
3

1 The products above are made by a company called Lichfield. What are they for? Can you describe them? Do you use them?

2 Match these descriptions to the items in **1**.

a It's dark blue and light blue.
b It weighs 1.6 kg.
c It's 2 m long.
d It's rectangular.
e It's 1.5 m high.
f It has two side pockets.

3 [3.5] Listen to a customer telephoning an outdoor equipment retailer. Tick (✓) the things in the first column that the caller asks about.

Description	Questions	Answers
Height	How high is it?	
Width	How .... is it?	
Weight	How .... is it?	
Size	How .... is it?	
Length ✓	How long is it?	It's 1 m 90.
Price	How .... is it?	
Material	What is it made of?	
Colour	What .... is it?	
Shape	What shape is it?	

4 [3.5] Work with a partner and complete the questions in the second column. Listen to the call again and complete the third column with the answers to the caller's questions.

5 You are a distributor of outdoor equipment in Italy. You would like to buy some Lichfield products. One of you should look at File 9 on page 60 and the other should look at File 27 on page 65.

QUICK CHECK

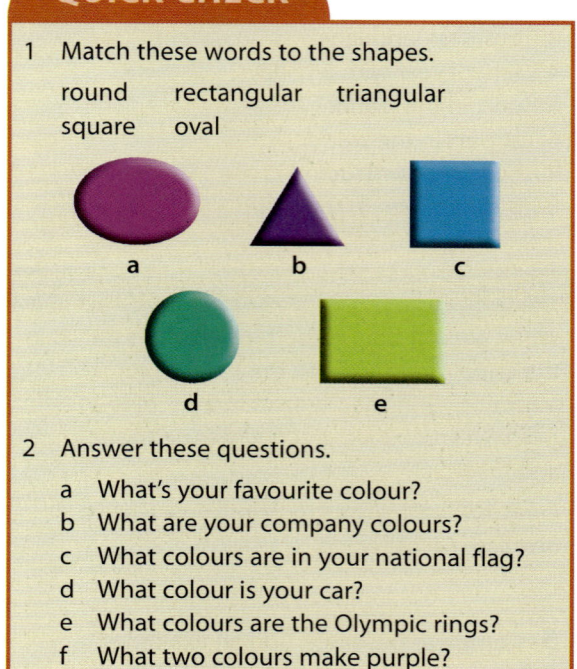

1 Match these words to the shapes.

round   rectangular   triangular
square   oval

a   b   c
d   e

2 Answer these questions.
  a What's your favourite colour?
  b What are your company colours?
  c What colours are in your national flag?
  d What colour is your car?
  e What colours are the Olympic rings?
  f What two colours make purple?

Task

Outdoor World is an exhibition which takes place every year. Work with a partner. Take it in turns to telephone the exhibition organizer to try and book a stand. The organizer needs to sell their stands. The buyer needs to get a stand within budget. One person should look at the information in File 1 on page 58 and the other should look at the information in File 7 on page 60.

ORGANIZING AN EVENT

1 Does your company organize events to celebrate special occasions? What kind of events does it have and what are the reasons for them?

2 Read the article about a company that organizes corporate events and answer these questions.

a What does Mark do?
b Who are his customers?
c Why is summer Mark's busiest period?
d How much room does he need to set up his game?

Mark Burghard runs Pulsar Laser Games. He organizes events for companies, sports clubs, and children's parties. The busiest time of the year for Mark is from Easter to October when the weather is good and the ground is dry. His equipment is very sophisticated but very easy to assemble and can be done very quickly in a large garden or small car park. Inside the tent people enter another world where the laser gun is king! So who are the most difficult customers? 'Funnily enough the adults are more difficult to control than the children,' says Mark.

3 [3.6] Listen to James Robertson trying to organize an event. Complete the table below.

Equipment available	
Dimensions	
Price	
Date	

4 [3.6] James asks some questions during the telephone call. Which ones can you remember? Listen again and check your answers.

e.g. Is that *Pulsar Laser*?

a Are you …?
b How big …?
c Sorry, did …?
d How much …?
e How long …?
f Could I …?

5 Work with a partner. One person should look at the information in File 6 on page 59 and the other should look at File 26 on page 65.

TASK

Work with a partner. It is the 25th anniversary of your company. You and a colleague from another office have to organize an event to celebrate the occasion.

1 You each have information about two possible venues. One person should look at the information in File 19 on page 63 and the other should look at the information in File 29 on page 66.

2 Call each other to exchange information about your choices and make notes. Agree to meet at a later date to make your final choice.

3 Have a meeting and compare the different places using your notes. Your budget is €2,000 for 40 people. Choose the best place to have the event.

4 Tell other groups what choice you made and explain why.

4 Getting things done

In this unit you are going to study ways of checking on progress and getting things done. You will:

check on the progress of a project

deal with complaints

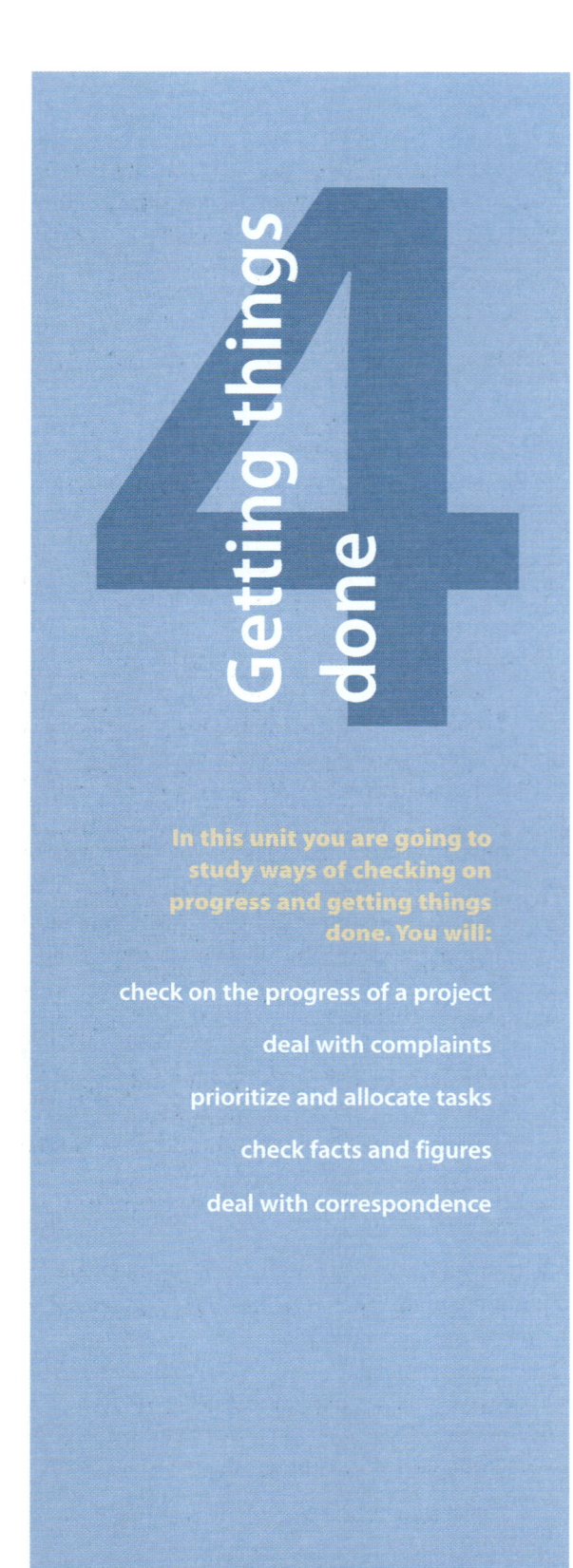

prioritize and allocate tasks

check facts and figures

deal with correspondence

> CHECKING PROGRESS

1 In a recent survey, people in Paris and London were asked how they spend their working day. Look at the results of the survey. Are you surprised? How is your time divided?

administrative tasks (filing, taking messages, printing documents, etc.)	36%
meetings/conversations with colleagues	20%
meetings/conversations with customers	18%
reading information	8%
having coffee	5%
thinking	8%
dealing with complaints	3%
making lists of things to do	2%

2 Look at these verbs and match them with the nouns in a–j below. Sometimes there is more than one answer.

send   do   make   arrange
pay   take   update   order

a   travel and hotel accommodation
b   phone calls
c   the filing
d   e-mails
e   the minutes for meetings
f   stationery
g   a database
h   invoices
i   messages
j   photocopies

3 Which of the tasks in **2** do you do? Do you enjoy them? Do you ask colleagues to do them?

4 ⟨4.1⟩ Charlie is replacing an employee who is on holiday for two weeks. He has a list of tasks to do. A colleague comes to see him to check his progress. Listen to the conversation and tick (✓) the tasks he has already done and put a cross (✗) next to things he hasn't done yet.

Date: 10/10

- ✗ Send invitations for press conference
- ✓ Arrange trip to Milan
- ✓ Do filing
- ✓ Call electrician
- ✗ Make photocopies for staff meeting
- ✗ Order stationery
- ✗ Do minutes of marketing meeting

Present perfect

When we are talking about recent past actions we often use the Present perfect.

I've arranged your trip for next week.
Have you sent the invitations? Yes, I have.
Has she done the minutes? No, she hasn't.

We use *not … yet* when we are still planning to do something.

I haven't phoned them yet. (I plan to do it this afternoon/tomorrow, etc.)

When we state the time of a past action, we normally use the Simple past.

He visited us last night.

5 Look at the list in **4** and complete these sentences with the correct form of the verb in brackets.

a Charlie .... invitations for the press conference. (send)
b He .... the trip to Milan. (arrange)
c He .... the filing. (do)
d He .... the photocopies for the staff meeting yet. (make)
e He .... the stationery. (order)

6 This is a list of action points from your team's last project meeting. It is now a week later and you've only had time to do five things on the list.

a Choose five items and tick (✓) them but do not let your partner see what you choose.

b Work with a partner and find out what they have/haven't done.

A *Have you booked your hotel room for the conference?*
B *No, I haven't yet. Have you booked yours?*

Minutes of NFS project team meeting
10 December

SUBJECT	ACTION/DECISION	
1 Conference	book hotel room	✓
2 Training	send training report to Personnel	✗
3 New product name	think of possible names	✓
4 Sales report	check own sales figures	✓
5 Database	update database with new client details	✗
6 Launch party	send invitations to main clients	✓
7 Invoices	pay November invoices	✓
8 Holiday requests	complete holiday forms for the year	✗

Task

1 Write a list of eight things you wanted to do this week – include things you have and haven't done.

2 Work with a partner. Give your list to your partner then take it in turns to ask your partner questions about their 'to do' lists.

A *Have you arranged a meeting with your main customer?*
B *No, not yet.*

▶ DEALING WITH COMPLAINTS

1 Do you complain a lot? Do people in your country complain a lot? What type of situations do you/they complain in?

2 Look at the cartoons. Who is talking to who? What do you think they're complaining about?

3 [4.2] Listen and match each conversation to one of the cartoons. What is the problem in each case?

> **to check out** to leave a hotel at the end of your stay
> **a delay** when something happens later than planned
> **heating** a system that makes a house, hotel, etc. warm

4 [4.2] Listen again and complete these sentences.

a A .... It's .... we are still waiting for new stock.
   B Oh, I see.
   A Right. Could I have your order number? .... just check your order.

b C My room's really cold.
   D .... I'm afraid we switched off all the heating last weekend. .... a technician to switch it on again.
   C .... I'm checking out at midday.

c F It's very noisy.
   E Yes, ..., sir. .... we have a school party on the flight.
   F I can see that.
   E .... if there's a seat free in business class?
   F ...., ... can I have another drink?
   E Certainly, sir.

5 Look at the conversations again. What expressions are used to apologize, to give reasons, and to make offers?

QUICK CHECK

Use these words to answer the questions below.

⊖ not very   fairly/quite   very   really ⊕

a How high is your salary?
b How difficult is it for you to write in English?
c How big is your apartment/house?
d How comfortable is your office?
e What do you think of your boss?
f What do you think about your job?
g How long is your journey to work?

6 Work with a partner. Have conversations for each of the problems a–d as in the example. Use the reasons and offers in *italics*.

A (Complaint:) *Your payment hasn't arrived.*
B (Apology:) *I'm very sorry about that.* (Reason:) *I'm afraid we have two people away in our accounts department.* (Offer:) *I'll send a cheque today.*
A (Acceptance:) *Thank you very much.*

a I think there is a mistake on my invoice.
   new person in the department → new invoice
b I'm going to miss my connecting flight because of this delay!
   fog at the airport → hotel for the night
c I've waited for two hours and you say there are no more tickets for the film.
   very popular film → free tickets for next week
d You sent an e-mail with the wrong attachment.
   new computer → send again

Task

Work with a partner. One person should look at the information below and the other should look at the information in File 33 on page 67.

1 Your cell phone company calls you to check you are happy with their service. Use the information below to reply. Complain when necessary.

- Your telephone is an old model. It's heavy.
- The messaging service is very slow.
- The network is good.
- You never make international calls because they are very expensive.
- You get a bill every three months. They are quite difficult to understand.
- You'd like information about new services.

2 You work for JTC, a holiday company. Your partner is one of your customers. Call your partner to check that they were satisfied with their holiday. If they are dissatisfied, offer them the special deals in the last column (*Action*). Complete the form below.

messaging service answerphone service on cell phones
a **network** a system of connections used by telecommunications services, e.g. cell phones, radios, etc.
welcome when guests are received in a friendly way

JTC CUSTOMER CARE FORM

Name: .... Destination: *Florida* Length of stay: *2 weeks*

	Very satisfied	Satisfied	Dissatisfied	Action (if problem)
Flight	☐	☐	☐	Give 20% off next flight
Welcome	☐	☐	☐	Send a free T-shirt
Hotel	☐	☐	☐	Offer one free night in a London hotel
Entertainment	☐	☐	☐	Send free CD
Food	☐	☐	☐	Give a free meal at *Pizza House*
JTC personnel	☐	☐	☐	Give 10% off next holiday
Check customer has received new brochure	YES ☐		NO ☐	Offer to send with free video

TASK MANAGEMENT

1 Are you involved in a new project at the moment? What are the different stages of the project? What stages are you responsible for?

2 ATC, a training company, is planning to open a computing school in Paris. Look at the list of tasks. Put them in order of priority (*1* = to do first, *9* = to do last). Then, work with a partner and compare your answers.

- ☐ Order furniture
- ☐ Choose premises
- ☐ Plan advertising and PR campaign
- ☐ Organize launch party
- ☐ Organize painting and building work
- ☐ Install telephones and computer network
- ☐ Get planning permission
- ☒ *1* Contact estate agents
- ☐ Recruit staff

estate agents people who sell property – houses, buildings, etc.
to install to put something in place
launch show something, e.g. a product, to the public for the first time
planning permission a licence to change the structure of a building
PR campaign a number of activities to attract public interest
premises buildings used by a company
to run to manage

3 [4.3] Listen to three managers at ATC discussing the Paris project.

a Do they mention all the tasks in **2**?
b What does Alberto ask Carla to do? What does he offer to do himself?

Task management

When we discuss the order to do tasks in, we use *need to* and *should*.

First of all, we **need to** find premises.
Then, we **should** do a new website in French.

When we ask someone to do something, we use *could you*?

Could you arrange the meeting for next week, please?

When we offer to do something we use *Shall I* or *I'll*.

Shall I organize the launch party?
I'll contact the estate agent.

4 Match each sentence in a–f to a sentence in 1–6. The same person is saying both sentences.

a I need to finish this report by lunchtime.
b You look very busy.
c We should advertise more.
d Only three people can come.
e We need someone to visit the factory in Wales.
f We need more price lists.

1 Shall I change the date?
2 Could you go?
3 I'll photocopy some.
4 Shall I give you a hand?
5 My boss is coming at 2 o'clock.
6 Could you find out some prices?

5 ATC's most important customer is visiting the company. Look at the schedule below. Your boss has asked you to share the job of looking after your visitor. Discuss who will do what.

A *One of us needs to meet her at the airport.*
B *Shall I do that?/I'm afraid I'm busy. Could you meet her?*

Thursday
21.30   Arrival Heathrow   *Who/meet?*

Friday
 9.00   Meeting with Financial Director
11.00   Visit resource centre   *Who/go with?*
13.00   Lunch with senior managers   *Who/book restaurant?*
15.00   Meeting with Design
18.00   Cocktail party   *Who/order drinks?*

Saturday
10.00   Visit new site   *Who/go with?*
14.00   Tennis tournament   *Who/take?*
17.30   Theatre   *Who/book tickets?*

Sunday
12.00   Leave from Heathrow   *Who/take?*

QUICK CHECK

Complete these sentences with one of these prepositions. Use each one once.

from   in   on   by   at   to   at   by

a   I flew to Munich .... 2nd April.
b   I attended a seminar on time management .... the weekend.
c   My report must be finished .... the end of the month.
d   I was on holiday .... Monday .... Wednesday.
e   Our management meeting is .... 9.30.
f   We do our budgets .... November so all figures must be ready .... 31st October.

Task

1 Work with one or two other people. You run a small new company. Look at the agenda for a meeting and the lists of things to do for each point on the agenda. Can you think of anything else? Add them to these lists.

1   Research trip to South America (you are all going):
    - *check database for contacts*
    - *choose countries to visit*

2   New publicity brochure:
    - *check prices*
    - *choose photographer*

3   Opening party:
    - *get invitations made*
    - *decide who to invite*

2 Hold a meeting and for each point decide and make a note of:
– what order to do the tasks in
– who should do each one.

A *First we need to check our database for contacts in South America. Could you do that?*
B *No problem. Then we should contact any useful people. Shall I do that, too?*

CHECKING FACTS

1 Where do you find information about hotels? What information do you like to know about them? Location, price, number of stars? Anything else?

2 Look at these advertisements for some hotels in Brussels.

a Which hotel is the cheapest?
b Which hotel is the closest to the Eurostar station?
c Which hotel has the most stars?
d Which hotel doesn't have a restaurant?
e Which is the largest hotel?

3 [4.4] One of the hotels receives a call. Which hotel is it? What information does the caller check? Make a note on the advertisement.

4 [4.4] Listen again and complete these sentences from the conversation

a …………… …………… …………… …………… …………… some details about your hotel.
b Your ad …………… you're eight minutes from the city centre. …………… …………… …………… ?
c …………… …………… by metro or on foot?
d Can …………… …………… …………… …………… your restaurant's open late at night?
e Yes, …………… …………… . Until 1 a.m.
f …………… …………… the nearest metro is Maclou?
g …………… , …………… …………… it's Louisa.
h The second night is free, …………… ?
i No, …………… …………… the third night that's free.
j …………… …………… …………… …………… the price for two, please?

Address http://www.metromag.com/hotels → go

Hotel Schuman
★★★

- Modern hotel in the heart of the city
- Conference facilities
- 10 minutes from central station
- 120 bedrooms all with en-suite shower or bath
- Private parking
- Double room from €82
- Excellent restaurant and bar
- All credit cards accepted

Tel: +32 (0)5453 1576
Fax: +32 (0)5453 1572

Hotel Soleil
★★

- Family hotel 5 minutes from city centre
- 15 minutes from Eurostar station
- Free breakfast
- 40 bedrooms some with en-suite shower
- €65 per person
- Great choice of restaurants 5 minutes away
- All credit cards accepted

Tel/Fax: +32 (0)5033 7856

Hotel Marguerite
★★★

- Comfortable hotel 8 minutes from city centre
- 10 minutes from Eurostar station
- 80 bedrooms with TV, telephone and minibar
- €60 per person
- €80 for two persons
- Restaurant open 11.30 a.m. till late

Tel: +32 (0)2513 9100
Fax: +32 (0)2513 9103

Third night free

5 Which of the expressions in **4** are used to check information? Which are used to confirm that the information is correct? And to correct information?

Checking and confirming information

To check information we can say:

I'd just like to check some details.
Could I just check that …?
You say/The ad says …, is that right?
Is that …
I suppose …
…, right?

To confirm/correct information, we can say:

Yes, that's right.
No, it's actually …/in fact …

To ask for confirmation, we can say:

Please could you just confirm …

6 Work with a partner. One of you works at the Hotel Soleil and the other works at the Hotel Schuman. Take it in turns to telephone and check information. One person should look at the information in File 31 on page 66 and the other should look at the information in File 35 on page 68.

QUICK CHECK

a How do you say these letters: A, E, I, O, U?

b How do you say these prices: £99, $125, €65.

c Put the days of the week in order and say them: T T W F S S M.

d Say these numbers: 1st, 2nd, 3rd, 4th. Continue to 10th.

e How many months end in -y? How many end in -r? What are the others?

f What is the date today? When is your birthday?

Task

Work with a partner. One of you should use the information on this page and the other should use the information in File 36 on page 68.

1 You are the Marketing Manager of a new hotel, the Meridien. Look at the message that your assistant took. When you return the call:

– check name of caller and how to spell it
– confirm he/she attended the press conference on 6th June
– check the name of the journalist's newspaper
– confirm his/her e-mail address
– check when the article will be in the newspaper.

2 Use the factsheet to answer your partner's questions.

Date and time: Wednesday, 12.35
Caller: Kay Hawkins
Re: Journalist from the Mail and Post. Was at press conference last week – wants more information for newspaper article on hotel. Please call back or fax info a.s.a.p.
Tel/Fax no: 0208 886532
E-mail: KHawkins@aol.com

Factsheet

Name of Hotel: Royal Meridien Dubai

- 5 star hotel; 1,000 beds
- Next to Jumeira beach
- $600 a night for a bedroom with views of the sea
- $400 a night in the rest of the hotel
- Rooms slightly cheaper in summer because temperature in summer is 50°C
- Health club has five hammam pools (hot Turkish-style baths)

SOLVING A PROBLEM

1 Look at this handout from a time management course. Is it good advice? Do you do any of these things?

MANAGING YOUR TIME

1. Every morning, write a 'to do' list for the day.
2. Divide long or difficult jobs into smaller tasks, and plan to do a little each day.
3. Start the day with short but urgent tasks.
4. Do easier tasks immediately after lunch.
5. Plan breaks in your day.
6. Learn to say 'no' when you're at work.
7. At the end of the day, check you've done all your tasks. If not, put them at the top of tomorrow's 'to do' list.

2 You work at a management training centre. Look at the letters and the e-mail and answer these questions.

a What is the letter from the bank about?
b Why is Mr Grand writing?
c Where is Charlotte?
d Why is Mr Larsen writing?
e What is Mr Platt's job?
f When is Henry leaving?
g How many people will attend the seminar in Sweden?
h How long was Mr Grand's course?

---

the **board** the people who control a company
a **mailshot** information sent to a large number of people at the same time
to be **overdrawn** to take more money out of your bank account than you really have
a **quotation** a statement of the cost of a product or service
a **refund** to get your money back
urgent needs to be done immediately

Dear Sir/Madam 24th March

I attended one of your courses last week on 'Time management'. Your brochure says, 'These two days will change your life'. In two days I learned nothing. I felt that the trainer was unprofessional and that the course was badly planned. I was also very disappointed with the hotel where the course took place. I would appreciate a full refund.

Yours truly,

Nicholas Grand
Nicholas Grand

❖ LBV Bank

Dear Sir/Madam 28th March

We notice that your current account is overdrawn by $450. Please could you check the situation. If you wish to discuss this matter, please telephone to arrange an appointment.

Yours sincerely

Phillip Platt
Phillip Platt
Manager

```
From:   LarsenSG
To:     P. Marshall
Date:   26 March
Re:     Three-day seminar
```

Dear Mr Marshall

We wish to arrange a three-day seminar on 'Marketing on the Internet'. Please could you send a quotation for a group of six managers? The course will take place at our headquarters in Malmo.

Yours

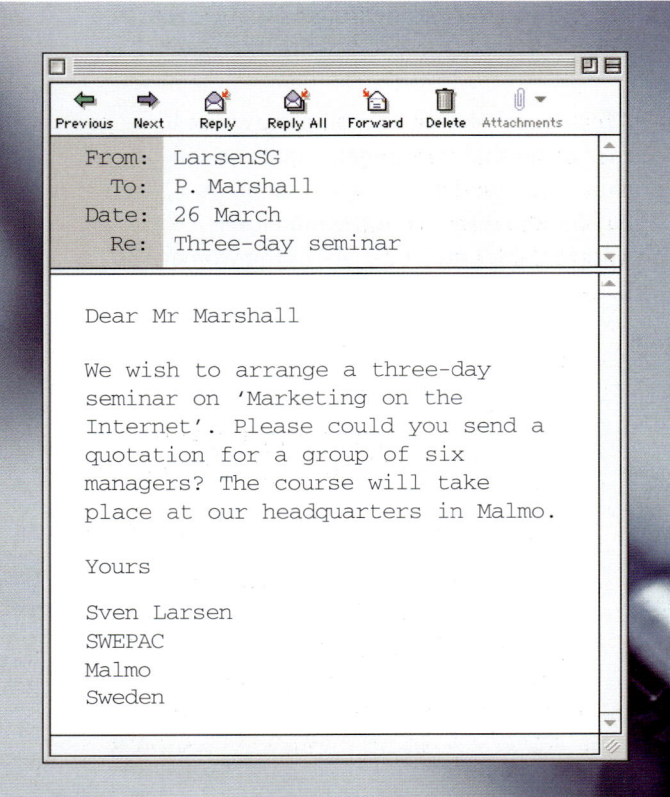

Sven Larsen
SWEPAC
Malmo
Sweden

Memo
29 March

Dear Peter

I will be away for a few days this week. Please could you do the following for me?
- Organize mailshot of new price list to all customers.
- Book restaurant for Henry's leaving party (his last day is 4th May).
- Send invitations.
- Pay March salaries.
- Telephone software company to arrange meeting for next Tuesday.
- Finish marketing report on Switzerland (for board meeting on 15th April).
- Check bank position and telephone if necessary.

Kindest regards

Charlotte

3 [4.5] Check your voicemail. There is one message for each letter or e-mail. Listen and make notes then answer these questions.
a   Why is Mr Grand calling?
b   What tasks has Charlotte done?
c   When will the seminar take place?
d   Is the situation at the bank worse or better?

Task

1 Work with a partner. Make a list of the things that need to be done, such as calling Nicholas Grand, booking a restaurant for Henry's leaving party, etc. Then, put them in order of priority.

To do
1
2
3
4
5
6
7

2 Now decide who should do each task. One of you is at a sales conference tomorrow and the day after (today is 2nd April). The other person is on holiday from 9–14th April.

3 One of the tasks on the 'to do' list is to telephone Nicholas Grand. Work in pairs and have the conversation. One person should look at File 23 on page 64 and the other should look at File 32 on page 66.

5 Planning ahead

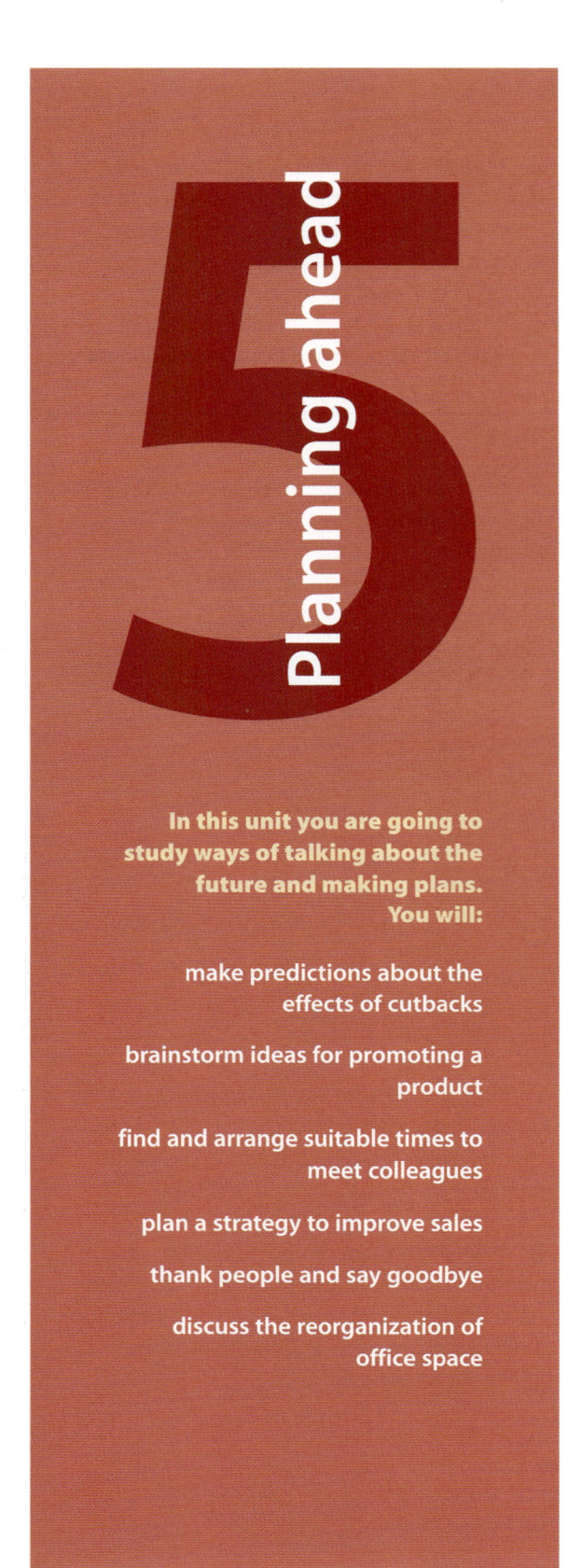

In this unit you are going to study ways of talking about the future and making plans. You will:

make predictions about the effects of cutbacks

brainstorm ideas for promoting a product

find and arrange suitable times to meet colleagues

plan a strategy to improve sales

thank people and say goodbye

discuss the reorganization of office space

> MAKING PREDICTIONS

1 Do you use the Internet for shopping? What do you buy? What else do you use the Internet for?

2 [5.1] An office supplies company wants to replace its normal printed catalogue with an on-line catalogue. Listen to two managers discussing the proposal. Is the man for or against the idea? And what about the woman?

3 [5.1] Listen again and match the first parts of each sentence a–e with the second parts 1–5. Which sentences are *for* the proposal and which ones are *against*?

a It'll
b I don't think it'll
c I think it'll
d It won't
e Customers will

1 save time for our customers.
2 be cheap.
3 be able to buy our latest products.
4 reduce our advertising costs.
5 work.

will and won't

We use *will/won't* to make predictions.
It **will**/It'**ll** be very expensive.
We **will**/We'**ll** need more staff.
It **won't** (**will not**) work.
On-line communications **won't** be free.

To express opinions about the future, we use
I think/don't think + will.
I think more companies **will** use the Internet.
I don't think customers **will** like it.

4 [5.1] Match each reason in 1–5 to an opinion in **3**. Listen again and check your answers. Practise giving the opinions and reasons.

e.g.
Customers will be able to buy our latest products because we'll be able to update our catalogue regularly.

1 we/be able/update/catalogue regularly ...e...
2 it/cost a lot/develop/website ....
3 customers/not like it ....
4 we/not have/send catalogues to all customers ....
5 customers/just press/a button to repeat their order ....

5 How will the Internet change life in the future? Here are some possible consequences. Tick (✓) *A* if you think this will happen and *B* if you don't think it will.

		A	B
a	All telecommunications will be free.	☐	☐
b	The personal computer (PC) will no longer exist.	☐	☐
c	Companies will only sell their products and services on-line.	☐	☐
d	Everybody will book their travel and holidays on the Internet.	☐	☐
e	The home-delivery industry will grow.	☐	☐
f	A lot of people will lose their jobs.	☐	☐

6 Discuss your answers with a partner. Explain your opinion, where possible.

I don't think all telecommunications will be free in the future. It'll be too expensive for the telecom companies. What do you think?

Task

Work with a partner. You work for a chain of supermarkets. Sales are down and running costs are up. You need to decide how to save or make some money.

1 Look at this memo. One person should write down one or two arguments *for* each idea and the other should write one or two arguments *against* each idea.

A TV advertising campaign will attract more customers. (argument for)
A TV advertising campaign will cost a lot. (argument against)

From: JBF
To: TG and HMC
Re: Ideas for saving/making money

Please could you look at these ideas and be prepared to discuss them at our next meeting on 5 March.

1 Launch a TV advertising campaign.
2 Open seven days a week instead of six.
3 Employ fewer staff.
4 Ask customers to pay for their plastic carrier bags.
5 Reduce prices on a hundred popular products by 10%.
6 Close one of the supermarkets in the town centre.

---

2 Hold a meeting with your partner and take it in turns to present your arguments to each other. When you have finished decide which are the three best ideas and tell the rest of the class why.

> IDEAS

1 To promote their products and services, companies can advertise on TV, offer free samples, or sponsor events. Can you add any other ideas? Which ones does your company use?

2 Read the text then answer these questions with a partner.

a What does Christopher Bartlett do?
b Who are his customers?
c What will happen at the special 'market days' at the brewery?
d Why would he jump off a bridge?
e Which of the ideas do you like most? Why?

CHEERS!

Christopher Bartlett is the owner of Brasserie de la Soif, a brewery in the west of France. He makes different traditional British beers, which he sells to local bars, pubs, and supermarkets.

Here are some of the ideas he has had for promoting his business:

- offering free beer tastings in local bars
- inviting local food producers to the brewery to sell their goods to the public on special 'market days'
- offering tours of the brewery
- putting up posters in bars
- having a competition to win a free tour of the brewery
- jumping off a bridge into the Loire river to promote new 'Willy Wolf' beer (Willy Wolf was a Polish acrobat who died jumping off the same bridge in 1925.)
- advertising the brewery on-line.

an **acrobat** a person who performs difficult physical acts
a **brewery** a place where beer is made
promote to give publicity to something to help to sell it
the **public** people in general
a **tasting** to drink something to try it before you buy it
a **tour** guided visits

3 [5.2] Listen to Christopher Bartlett and his partner discussing the promotional ideas. Which of the ideas in the text in **2** do they discuss?

4 [5.2] Listen again and complete these sentences.

a .... about .... to bars in the evening and .... customers free tastings?
b .... we .... free tours of the brewery?
c We .... the local radio station.

5 [5.2] Listen again and match these responses to the suggestions in **4**.

1 I'm not really sure about that. ....
2 That's a great idea. ....
3 That's not a bad idea. ....

Making suggestions

To suggest ideas, we can say:

Why don't we have a competition?
How/What about mailing companies?
We could visit local supermarkets.

To respond to suggestions we can say:

That's a great idea/not a bad idea.
I'm not sure about that.

6 Work with a partner. You are opening a new restaurant in the town centre. Take it in turns to suggest and respond to the ideas below.

A *Why don't we offer free tastings in the street.*
B *That's a great idea. We could do that in front of the restaurant.*

– offer free tastings in the street
– invite a journalist from the local newspaper
– start a home-delivery service
– sponsor a local sports club
– have a website
– do a mailshot to offices in the town centre

Task

Work with a partner. Your company is launching a new product called Life Force. Life Force is a special high-energy sweet for people who do sport. You need to decide how to promote this new product. One person should look at the information below. The other should look at File 39 on page 69.

These are some ideas you have for promoting and advertising new Life Force sweets.

a sponsor a big football team – Life Force logo on players' shirts for 1 year
   Cost: €5 million
b advertise in sports and health magazines – place 36 half-page ads in 6 different magazines
   Cost: €4.5 million
c sponsor some sports projects – give money to build sports facilities in big cities
   Cost: €2 million
d organize a national competition – offer 50 prizes of a skiing holiday for two
   Cost: €1 million (not including advertising)

1 Make your suggestions to your partner and listen to your partner's suggestions.

2 You have a total advertising budget for the year of €15 million. Decide which ideas to choose.

You can start like this:

Why don't we sponsor a big football team? For €5 million we could have our logo on players' shirts for a year.

ARRANGEMENTS

1 Do you know what your plans are for the rest of this week? This month? This year?

2 Look at the e-mail and the schedule and answer these questions.

a Why is Ewart Carson writing to Simon O'Mullane?
b What seminars are already arranged?
c What dates are still free?
d Which speakers does Ewart Carson still need to contact?
e Are the seminars in the morning or the evening?

3 [5.3] Ewart Carson calls Simon O' Mullane about his talk. Listen and write the time and title of the talk in the right place on the schedule.

4 [5.3] Listen again and complete these sentences.

a I'm sorry, but .... away that weekend.
b No, I'm afraid someone else .... on that day.
c What .... later in the month?

5 Work with a partner. Tell your partner about your plans for this weekend and for next week.

6 [5.3] Match the first parts of each sentence or question a–g with the second parts 1–7. Then listen again and check your answers.

a When
b Are you free
c How about
d Friday 27th
e Is
f Well, I'd prefer
g So that's

1 is fine.
2 six o'clock OK?
3 are you free?
4 on Friday 13th?
5 Thursday of that week?
6 Friday 27th at six, then.
7 a little later if possible.

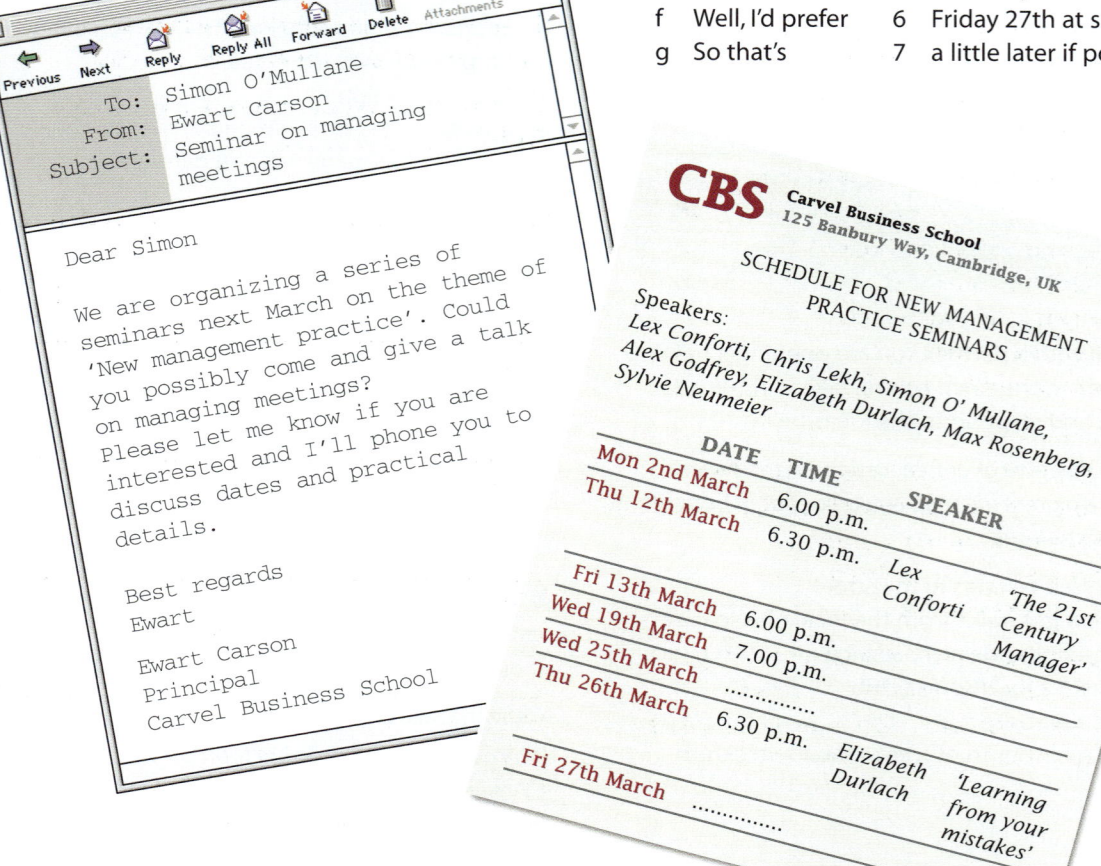

To: Simon O'Mullane
From: Ewart Carson
Subject: Seminar on managing meetings

Dear Simon

We are organizing a series of seminars next March on the theme of 'New management practice'. Could you possibly come and give a talk on managing meetings? Please let me know if you are interested and I'll phone you to discuss dates and practical details.

Best regards
Ewart

Ewart Carson
Principal
Carvel Business School

CBS Carvel Business School
125 Banbury Way, Cambridge, UK

SCHEDULE FOR NEW MANAGEMENT PRACTICE SEMINARS

Speakers: Lex Conforti, Chris Lekh, Simon O' Mullane, Alex Godfrey, Elizabeth Durlach, Max Rosenberg, Sylvie Neumeier

DATE	TIME	SPEAKER	
Mon 2nd March	6.00 p.m.		
Thu 12th March	6.30 p.m.	Lex Conforti	'The 21st Century Manager'
Fri 13th March	6.00 p.m.		
Wed 19th March	7.00 p.m.		
Wed 25th March			
Thu 26th March	6.30 p.m.	Elizabeth Durlach	'Learning from your mistakes'
Fri 27th March	....		

Future plans

We use the Present continuous tense to talk about and ask about planned future actions.

*What **are** you **doing** tonight? I**'m meeting** friends for a drink.*
*What **is** (What**'s**) he **doing** tomorrow? He**'s going** away for the weekend.*

To check when someone is available, we can say:

When are you free?
Are you free on Monday/in the afternoon?

To suggest a time or a date, we can say:

***How/What about** Tuesday?*
Is 3 p.m. OK?

To tell someone we are or aren't free, we can say:

Yes, that's fine.
I'm afraid I'm busy/not free then.
I'm sorry, but I'm working late, etc.

To confirm an arrangement, we can say:

So, that's 11 a.m. on Monday 4 May, then.

7 Work with a partner. One person should look at the information in File 25 on page 65. The other should look at the information in File 30 on page 66.

Task

Work with a partner. You've agreed to take part in an experiment for learning English on the Internet. You need to find 12 hours next week that you can both attend lessons.

1 Fill in your diary opposite with these details. Tick the boxes when you have filled them in.

– three meetings of two hours ☐
– two half-day visits ☐
– a business lunch and dinner ☐
– two sports activities ☐
– a doctor's appointment ☐

Remember that:

– you can only do the lessons at your desk
– you can't have more than 2 hours per lesson
– there is a maximum of 4 hours per day
– lessons are Monday to Friday only
– all lessons are between 8 a.m. and 7 p.m.

2 Try to arrange 12 hours of lessons with your partner/s. Change appointments or meetings that are less important or less urgent (e.g. sports activities).

3 When you have finished, check all your arrangements with your partner, like this:

So, we're having a two-hour lesson on .... from .... to ....

Mon
Tue
Wed
Thur
Fri

▶ FUTURE PLANS

1 What car do you drive? When did you buy it? Why did you choose it? What's your dream car?

2 Read the text below and answer these questions.

a What is Aston Martin's problem?
b Why does the company have this problem?
c What is the company doing to solve the problem?

ASTON MARTIN BUILDS FOR THE FUTURE

What do Sir Elton John, the Sultan of Brunei and Prince Charles have in common? The answer is that they all own a number of Aston Martins, the car that was first made famous in the James Bond film *Goldfinger*. The Aston Martin is many people's dream car, but the company has never made a profit. The cars sell for a lot of money, but they don't make many of them. The new Vanquish V12 model, for example, is made mainly by hand in the company's Newport Pagnell factory. The car sells for around £200,000, but the factory only produces about 300 of these vehicles a year. Their other factory at Bloxham produces the DB7 Convertible and Coupé models at a rate of only 38 per week.

But things are changing at Aston Martin Lagonda, and the company hopes to make a profit very soon. It is going to launch a new lower-price car, a 'baby' Aston or roadster. As a manager explains: 'We're going to open a new production centre for the new car in Graydon. In three years we plan to have an annual production of 3,500 roadsters. Total annual production will be more than 5,000 cars, compared with about 1,000 now.'

Aston also plans to double its network of sixty dealers around the world. Maybe there'll be one near you. If you're interested, the new lower-price 'baby' Aston will cost you between £60,000 and £90,000!

---

at a rate of the speed at which something happens
to double to make twice as big
to have something in common to have the same characteristics or interests
network of dealers a group of companies that sell cars
roadster a small sports car

---

3 Complete this table using the information in the text.

	Now	The future
Number of production plants		
Car models	DB7 convertible + coupé Vanquish V12	
Number of cars produced		
Number of dealers		
Typical price	Vanquish V12: £...............	

4 Underline the verbs in the text that are used to talk about the company's future plans.

e.g.
… the company <u>hopes</u> to make a profit very soon.

Plans and objectives

We use *going to* to talk about a *definite* plan of action.

We**'re going to** open a new factory in June.
He**'s going to** recruit a new technician this month.

We can use *plan to* and *hope to* to talk about objectives or targets. We use *plan to* when we are more certain and *hope to* when we are less certain.

They **plan to** double their sales in two years.
He **hopes to** finish the report before the end of the week.

5 Work with a partner. Use the information in **3** and take it in turns to talk about the present and future situation. Use *going to* to talk about the company's plans.

e.g.
The company only has two factories at present. It's going to open a third factory.

6 Match the problems in a–f with the solutions in 1–6 below.
a Customers have a long wait when they call our company.
b Most people in our company are over forty years old.
c Our factory is too small.
d Our customers complain that products don't arrive on time.
e Our products sell well, but not in big quantities.
f Last month one per cent of our products had technical defects.

1 Employ more university graduates. (How many?)
2 Build a new factory. (Where?)
3 Have more customer service lines. (How many?)
4 Find a new transport company. (When?)
5 Offer a discount on large orders. (How much?)
6 Improve quality control. (How?)

7 Work with a partner. Have conversations about the situations in **6**. Use the words in brackets to continue the conversation like this.

A *Customers have a long wait when they call our company.*
B *So what are you going to do?*
A *We're going to have more customer service lines.*
B *How many do you plan to install?*
A *We hope to have five lines.*

Task

Work with a partner. You are both managers for a national daily newspaper, *The Word*.

1 Read the memo from the CEO of your company.
a What are the present problems?
b With your partner decide what to do. Think about these points:
- target market
- design (use of colour, photos, etc.)
- contents (balance of sports/economic news, etc.)
- price of newspaper
- new targets (sales, advertising, etc.).

e.g.
I think we should (have more political stories).
I don't think we should (increase the price).
Why don't we …?

FAST TRACK PUBLISHING
Memorandum

To: Senior Managers

Three years ago *The Word* sold 175,000 copies a day. Now we sell 100,000 and sales are still falling. In this three-year period, advertising revenue has gone down from $200,000 a month to less than $80,000. 67% of the population say that *The Word* is boring and old-fashioned. The average age of our readers is now 51! We urgently need new ideas. There will be a meeting this Wednesday at 10.00 a.m to discuss the situation.

Rupert Butcher

---

2 Present your ideas. The group with the best ideas will keep their jobs!

e.g.
We're going to (use more photos).
We plan to/hope to (increase sales by 20% in the first year).

STAYING IN TOUCH

1 Do you stay in touch with new people that you have met at conferences or visits to companies? Why?

2 Roberta Heymann is from New York. She is visiting Gianluca Fiorini in Rome on business. Look at the sentences below the picture.

a Who is speaking in each case, Roberta or Gianluca?
b What did they do this morning?
c What are they doing for the rest of the day?

a *See you at your hotel at 7 o'clock.*

b *It was nice to meet everybody.*

c *Thank you for inviting me.*

d *Have a nice afternoon at the Coliseum.*

3 [5.4] Match these responses to the sentences in **2**. Then listen and check.

a I'm glad you enjoyed it.
b Thank you very much.
c Yes, see you later.
d You're welcome.

4 Work with a partner. Complete each sentence a–d with three expressions from 1–12 below. Can you think of more ways to complete each sentence?

a It was ………, ………, ………
b Have a ………, ………, ………
c Thank you for ………, ………, ………
d See you ………, ………, ………

1 coming.
2 next year.
3 everything.
4 good trip back.
5 again soon.
6 nice weekend.
7 nice to see you again.
8 pleasant lunch.
9 tomorrow.
10 a wonderful evening.
11 having me.
12 an interesting visit.

5 Match the sentences you made in **4** with these possible responses.

1 I look forward to it.
2 And you.
3 It was a pleasure.
4 I'm glad I could help.
5 Thanks.
6 I'm glad you enjoyed it.
7 Yes, I hope so.
8 You too.
9 You're welcome.

6 [5.5] Listen to these eight short conversations. Is the response correct (✓) or incorrect (✗)? Suggest a better response where necessary.

a ………   e ………
b ………   f ………
c ………   g ………
d ………   h ………

Saying goodbye

We can use these expressions when we say goodbye:

Thank you for all your help/ showing me round.
It was a useful visit.
Response: *It was a pleasure./You're welcome. I'm glad I could help/you enjoyed it.*
It was nice to see you again/to meet you.
Response: *And you.*
Have a nice weekend/safe journey back.
Response: *Thanks. You too.*
See you next week/in March.
Speak to you tomorrow/soon.
Response: *Yes, I hope so./I look forward to it.*

Notice that we use *meet* when it was our first face-to-face contact with the person. We use *speak to* when our next contact will be by phone.

7 [5.6] Now you will hear eight sentences. Listen and respond to each one.

QUICK CHECK

Do you know the difference between *travel*, *trip*, and *journey*? Complete a–e with one of these words.

a   How was your .... to Canada?
b   Did you .... by tram or bus?
c   How long does the .... from Paris take?
d   What are your .... plans for next year?
e   How many business .... do you go on in a year?

Task

Work with a partner. Have conversations for the following situations. When you have finished, change roles. Make sure you give appropriate responses.

Situation 1
After a presentation: host and guest speaker

Host
- Thank your guest for coming
- Respond and comment on presentation – very interesting
- Invite your guest for dinner this evening and fix a time

Guest
- Respond and comment on audience – very interested
- Respond and comment on presentation room – comfortable
- Confirm time and place for dinner

Situation 2
End of company visit: host and visitor

Visitor
- Thank your host for your tour of the factory
- Ask time of meeting tomorrow
- Say you will see your host at that time
- Respond

Host
- Respond
- Say time: 9.30 a.m.
- Respond and wish your visitor a nice evening

Situation 3
End of a phone call between two colleagues

Colleague A
- Thank your colleague for their help
- Thank your colleague and respond
- Respond

Colleague B
- Respond and wish your colleague a good weekend
- Tell A you will see them at next week's meeting

Situation 4
End of annual conference:
two participants – A is there for first time

Participant A
- Comment on conference – very useful
- Say you were happy to meet the other participants
- Respond and wish them a good journey back

Participant B
- Respond and comment on conference – better last year
- Respond and say you hope to see A next year
- Thank them

MAKING CHOICES

1 The pictures show three ways of saving office space in a company. Match the pictures to the descriptions a–c below.

a   Hot-desking: Employees share an office or desk. They only use it for one or two days a week when they are in the company.
b   Open-plan offices: Employees work in one big office, not in individual offices.
c   Teleworking: Employees work at home and communicate with their company by computer or telephone.

2 Do you think these are good ways of working? Why/Why not? Does your company do anything similar?

3 [5.7] Listen to a CEO discussing ways of creating more office space with two senior managers. Does the company need more office space in Manchester or in London? Why?

4 [5.7] Listen again and complete these sentences.

a   As you know, ... our Manchester office in December.
b   We .... the Customer Service Department to London.
c   .... the number of people that use the London offices.

5 Does your company or a company you know have plans for moving offices or moving staff? Tell a partner.

We're (verb + -ing) …
We plan/hope to …
We're going to …

6 [5.8] Listen to the three managers suggesting ways of finding more office space. Write their suggestions and the disadvantages they mention in the table.

Suggestion	Disadvantages
Make offices open-plan.	It'll be expensive.

7 Work with a partner. Make and respond to the suggestions in **6**.

A   *Why don't we make our offices open-plan?* (suggestion)
B   *It'll be very expensive.* (disadvantage)
A   *I disagree. I don't think it'll be expensive.* (agrees or disagrees)

8 [5.9] Listen to the three managers arranging a time for their next meeting. Write the day and the time of the next meeting.

9 [5.9] Choose the correct word or expression in *italics*. Then listen again and check your answers.

a When *are/do* you free?
b How *free/about* Tuesday afternoon?
c I'm *sorry/afraid*, but I'm going to Munich that day.
d *Say/How* 9.30?
e Thank you *to come/for coming* today.
f *Have/Enjoy* a good weekend.
g *Have/See* you next Thursday at 9.30.

10 Work with a partner. One person should look at the information in File 8 on page 60 and the other should look at the information in File 28 on page 65.

Task

Work with a partner. You need to find offices on the same floor for ten staff from your Sales and Customer Service Department. You only have eight offices, so staff who are only in the office a few days a week will have to share an office.

1 Each of you has different information about four of the staff. One person should use the information in File 13 on page 61 and the other should use the information in File 17 on page 62. Exchange this information and complete the table below, as for Nick and Steve, like this:

When does Delphine work? What's her job? Does she need a computer? Are there any other things we need to think about?

2 Look at the floor plan and make suggestions about where to put each person.

3 Present your solution to the rest of the class.

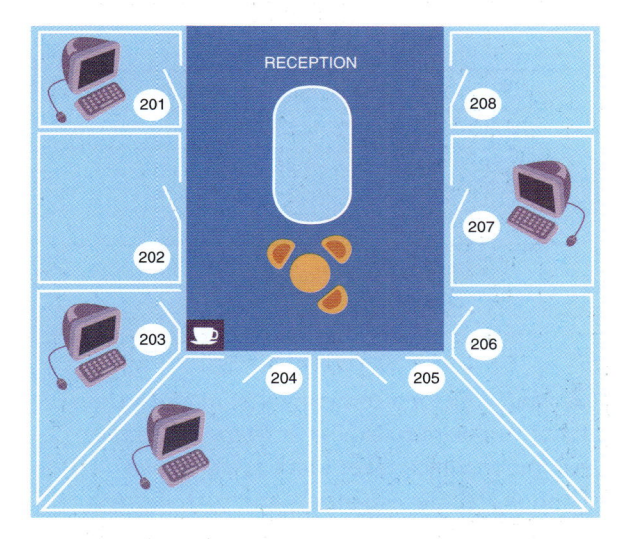

	Nick	Delphine	Petra	Maya	Ulrich	Steve	John	Robert	Paula	Tanya
Mon	✓					✓				
Tue	✓					✓				
Wed	✓					✓				
Thu	✓					✓				
Fri	✓					✓				
Need computer	✓					✓ all the time				
Job	Sales Manager					Administrator				
Other info	PA nearby					coffee and chats with Petra				

Information files

FILE 1

Unit 3 Product details Task, p34

1 You work for an exhibition organizer. *Outdoor World* is an exhibition which takes place every year in London. When your partner calls you, use this information.
You have sold all the stands except these three.

Stand A	3 m x 3 m; rental: €8,000
Stand B	4 m x 3 m; rental: €9,500
Stand C	5 m x 3 m; rental: €12,000
Furniture	Tables €200 Chairs €100 Telephone €150

You could offer a discount of 10% on Stands B or C.

2 You work for a company that manufactures tents. You want to exhibit at *Outdoor World,* an exhibition which takes place every year in London. Call the organizers and try to book a stand. Use this information.

- Any stands available?
- Your total budget is €12,000.
- You want one table for your brochures and two chairs. Check the price.
- You want a space to put up one of your tents. It is 240 cm x 120 cm.
- You want a television and VCR. Check the price.
- Ask for the total price.

FILE 2

Unit 3 Making comparisons Task, p33

	Option 1 Oxford, England	Option 2 Leiden, Holland	Option 3 Chantilly, France
Population	150,000	80,000	10,000
Student population (16+)	18,000	20,000	2,000
Shop available	In town centre	In commercial centre near Leiden	In town centre
Other cities	London 60 km	Amsterdam 30 km	Paris 40 km
Size	80 m²	140 m²	240 m²
Rent per m²	€200 m²/year	€400 m²/year	€100 m²/year
Employment rates	€8 per hour	€9 per hour	€10 per hour
Lease	3 years	1 year	5 years
Delivery	Difficult during office hours	Easy	Easy

FILE 3

Unit 2 Company overview 5, p27

a First South Korea, then China.
b Frankfurt.
c Because the car industry was growing.
d Drugs, agricultural chemicals, etc.
e A light-weight, white synthetic material used in food packaging and for insulation in houses.
f Europe, North and South America, and the Far East.
g Industrial dyes.

FILE 4

Unit 1 Asking for information Task, p7

1 You are a hotel guest and you want this information. Ask your partner questions.

- Bureau de change in the hotel? Where? What time/open/close?
- Restaurant in hotel? Where? What time/open/evening?
- Buses from airport? What time/leave/arrive?
- Where/breakfast room? What time/breakfast/start/finish?

2 You are a receptionist at a hotel. Your partner is a guest. Look at this information and answer your partner's questions.

GUEST INFORMATION

Business Centre Open 7.30 a.m. – 8.00 p.m. every day for all your business needs: computers, e-mail, fax, etc.

Newspapers A wide selection of national and international newspapers in the Guest Lounge (see plan). Available from 6.15 a.m. every morning.

Entertainment In hotel: Midnight Sounds jazz club (see plan). Concerts 9.30 – 11.30 p.m.
Near hotel: BJ's Night Club – jazz and blues. Behind hotel in Clinton Street.

Telephones Telephones on every floor (coins or phone card). Credit card telephones in Clinton Street.

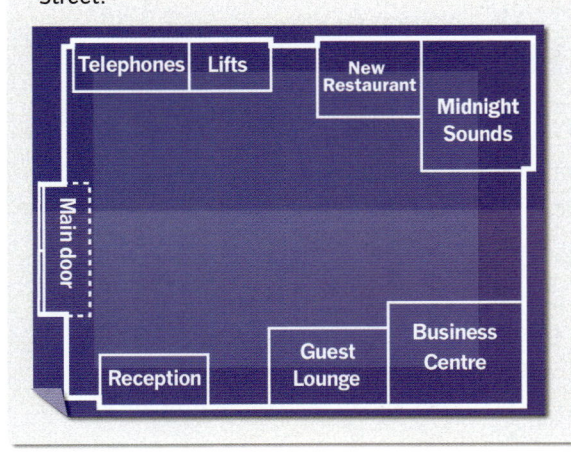

[Plan showing: Telephones, Lifts, New Restaurant, Midnight Sounds, Main door, Reception, Guest Lounge, Business Centre]

FILE 5

Unit 1 Requests 4, p8

1 Listen to your partner's description of two companies. Write down the name, where the head office is, the telephone number, and website address for each company. Ask your partner to spell words where necessary.

2 Give your partner the details of these two companies. You can start like this:

The first company is Toshiba. The head office is in Tokyo, Japan …

Company name	Toshiba	Bang & Olufsen
Head office	Tokyo, Japan	Struer, Denmark
Tel. number	3457 2096	96 84 11 22
Website	www.toshiba.co.jp	www.bang-olufsen.com

FILE 6

Unit 3 Organizing an event 5, p35

It is 25 April. You want to organize the laser event for your staff. Your partner works for Pulsar Laser. Call them and check the following information. Then make a booking if possible.

Check size – height and surface area. You have a car park: 20 m × 30 m.

Dates? Your preferences are now 2nd May, 7th May, or 13th May.

Number of people to invite – want to invite 80 people.

Duration of show – have to be finished by midnight and cannot start until 8 p.m.

Cost per person or per hour? Have a budget of £600.

Deposit – when? How much? Cancellation charges?

Booking – check price and date and time and make a booking if possible.

FILE 7

Unit 3 Product details Task, p34

1 You work for an outdoor clothing company. You want to exhibit at *Outdoor World*, an exhibition which takes place every year in London. Call the organizers and try to book a stand. Use this information.

- Any stands available?
- Your total budget is €10,000.
- You need an area of 10–15 m².
- You want one table for your brochures, price lists, and general information. Check the price.
- You want a second table to receive customers and two chairs. Check the price.
- You want a telephone. Check the price.
- Ask for the total price.

2 You work for an exhibition organizer. *Outdoor World* is an exhibition which takes place every year in London. When your partner calls, use this information. You have sold all the stands except three.

Stand A	3 m x 3 m; rental: €8,000
Stand B	4 m x 3 m; rental: €9,500
Stand C	5 m x 3 m; rental: €12,000.
Furniture	Tables €200 Chairs €100 TV/VCR €400

You could offer a discount of 10% on Stands B or C.

FILE 8

Unit 5 Making choices 10, p57

You are the CEO. You're not free for the meeting next Thursday. Call and arrange another time for the following week. You are free all day Tuesday and Wednesday, or on Friday before 1.30 p.m.

FILE 9

Unit 3 Product details 5, p34

1 You work for Lichfield. Your partner, who is a distributor, calls you and asks for information about the items below. Use the information to answer their questions.

Arran Rucsacs

	Arran 60+	Arran 85
Size	60 litres	85 litres
Weight	1.6 kg	1.9 kg
Colour	Green/Black Blue/Black	Green/Black Blue/Black
Price	€55	€75
Material	PVC coated fabric	PVC coated fabric

2 You are a distributor and want to sell Lichfield tents in your region. Your partner works for Lichfield. Call them and ask for the information below. You are interested in the Inca brand of tents.

	Inca 1800	Inca 2400
Size (packed)		
Weight		
No. of people		
Price		
Colour		

FILE 10

Unit 2 Systems and processes 1, p24

1. False. It's about 71%.
2. True.
3. True. Even if we reduce it by 5%, we will be very ill.
4. True. Tap water often contains chlorine.
5. True.
6. False. Bottled water is in sixth position, after soft drinks, beer, milk, coffee, fruit juices, and fruit drinks.

FILE 11

Unit 2 Facts and figures 8, p19

Ask your partner questions about the company in column A and complete the table. Use the information in column B to answer your partner's questions.

	A	B
Name of company	....	Domino Printing
Activity	produces	manufactures equipment to print information on boxes or bottles
Turnover	about €............... billion	about £140 million
Number of employees	....	1,400
Sites	Operates .... nuclear reactors and .... uranium production sites in France	head office in Cambridge and factory in California
Interesting fact	nuclear power provides .... of France's electricity	exports 88% of its products

FILE 12

Unit 2 Personal profiles 8, p23

Ask your partner questions to find the missing information.
e.g. *When was she born?*

....	Born in Belgium.
1939	Family moves to ....
1946	Returns to Europe to study art.
....	Finishes her studies.
	Wins a .... in New York.
1951	Gets a job as a clothes designer in New York.
	Later joins Jonathan Logan as a chief designer.
....	Leaves Jonathan Logan and creates ....
1980	Wins the award of ....
....	Her company goes public.
1986	Company is in 'Fortune 500' list for the first time.
1987	Becomes ....

an **award**   a prize
to **go public**   to be listed on the stock market for the first time

FILE 13

Unit 5 Making choices Task, p57

Delphine Turlier (Customer Service Manager)
She reports to the Sales Manager. She spends Monday and Tuesday in another branch. She works on her laptop computer.

Maya Ducanec (Personal Assistant to Sales Manager)
She's been with the company for 25 years. She has always had her own office. She uses the computer all the time. She works from Monday to Friday.

Robert Fischer (Sales Representative)
He's usually in the office on Tuesday and Thursday. He has a laptop computer. He sometimes comes in on Fridays.

Tanya Dalton (Customer Service Assistant)
She spends two days a week at home and three days in the office. She can come to the office any day(s) of the week. She works on her laptop all the time.

FILE 14
Unit 3 Telephoning 3, p28

1 Call your partner to get their company's fax number.

- Introduce yourself.
- Say where you are calling from and why.
- Thank the person at the other end.

2 You receive a call from your partner.

- Answer the phone and give your company name (Senkay Electric). Offer to help.
- Note down the name of the caller.
- Your website address is: www.senkaye.com.

FILE 15
Unit 2 Personal profiles 8, p23

Ask your partner questions to find the missing information.

e.g. *Where was she born?*

1929	Born in ....
1939	Family moves to America.
1946	Returns to Europe to study ....
1950	Finishes her studies.
	Wins a fashion design competition in New York.
1951	Gets a job as a clothes designer in ....
	Later joins .... as a chief designer.
1976	Leaves Jonathan Logan and creates Liz Claiborne Inc.
....	Wins the award of 'Entrepreneurial Woman of the Year'.
1981	Her company goes public.
....	Company is in 'Fortune 500' list for the first time.
1987	Becomes Chairman and CEO of company.

an **award**   a prize
to **go public**   to be listed on the stock market for the first time

FILE 16
Unit 1 Friendly welcomes Task, p11

Your partner is coming to present a report at your company. Meet your partner and show them to the conference room. Be ready to offer help. Before the conversation, decide what to say for each point below. Follow the example. During the conversation, listen carefully to your partner and respond to the things they say.

- Greet your visitor.
  Hello. Nice to see you again. How are you?
- Thank your visitor for coming.
- Walk with your visitor to the conference room.
- Go into the conference room – explain that it has space for 100 people.
- Ask if your visitor wants to open a window.
- Say that 50 people are coming to the presentation. Offer to make more copies.
- Offer your visitor the use of your phone.

FILE 17
Unit 5 Making choices Task, p57

Petra Darling (Sales Assistant)
She comes into the office from Monday to Wednesday each week. She works on a computer most of the time.

Ulrich Schmidt (Sales Representative)
He's in the office every Monday, then either Wednesday or Thursday. He has a laptop.

John Cowles (Customer Service Assistant)
He works in the office from Monday to Friday. He spends most of his time on the phone and looking up information on his computer. He doesn't like any noise in or near his office.

Paula Amano (Sales Representative)
She's in the office every Thursday and Friday. She needs to use a computer when she is at work.

FILE 18

Unit 3 Telephoning Task, p29

1 Call your partner and find out the following information about ITC. Check it carefully! Introduce yourself at the start of the call. Get the information and end the call politely.

- Introduce yourself.
- Discount on hotels? How much?
- Cheap flights?
- Website? On-line booking?

2 Your partner calls you for information on ITC.

- Answer the phone and give your name.
- ITC offers up to 30% discount on car rental.
- The first three months is free, then monthly payment.
- ITC offers €100,000 free travel insurance.

FILE 19

Unit 3 Organizing an event Task, p35

You have got information about two places for your company's event. Call your partner and exchange information. Your partner has information about two other places. Ask your partner about them and make notes.

	Country Hotel	Nightclub
Name	Redwood Lodge	Caesars!
No. of people	60	150
Distance from head office	40 km	5 km
Food	Hot buffet	Snack
Drink	Free wine	2 free drinks Drinks €5
Opening hours	8–12 p.m.	9 p.m.–3 a.m.
Cost per person	€40/head	€25/head
Special offers	Free pianist	Games and competitions organized

FILE 20

Unit 1 Describing jobs 8, p13

1 Listen to your partner's description and draw the organization chart.

2 Now describe this chart to your partner, who will draw it. You are the Sales Manager.

e.g.
I'm the Sales Manager. I manage eight people. I report to …

```
                    CEO
                     |
            Sales Director
         develops business
             for company
              /        \
   Sales Manager      Export Manager
 • develops sales   • global exports
   in Europe        • team of 12 people
 • team of 8 people
```

FILE 21

Unit 1 Requests 4, p8

1 Give your partner the details of these two companies. You can start like this:

The first company is Ericsson. The head office is in Stockholm, Sweden …

Company name	Ericsson	Samsung
Head office	Stockholm, Sweden	Seoul, South Korea
Tel. number	8 719 00 00	3706 1114
Website	www.ericsson.se	www.samsungcorp.com

2 Listen to your partner's description of two other companies. Write down the name, where the head office is, the telephone number, and website address for each company. Ask your partner to spell words if necessary.

FILE 22

Unit 2 Current activities 7, p21

Ask your partner questions to find out the missing information and answer your partner's questions.

e.g. *Who is Angela training?*

JOHNSON, OLSON & BRONSON

Staff schedule for today
Tuesday, 7 July

HUMAN RESOURCES
Angela – training ....
Björn – interviewing candidates for R & D job

SALES AND MARKETING
Peter – making a presentation to ....
Valerie – visiting customers

FINANCE
Angus – finishing annual report (no interruptions please)
Melissa – preparing ....

IT
Patrick – developing new ....
Sophia – meeting new suppliers

R & D
Maria – testing of BM46 prototype
Thomas – ....

FRONT OFFICE
Sarah – welcoming .... visitors
William – answering phone

FILE 23

Unit 4 Solving a problem Task, p45

1 You work for the management training centre. Call Nicholas Grand about his letter of complaint. Check the following information.

– Check the course dates (24–26 February).
– Check the name of the trainer (Tim Watts).
– Check the cost ($450).
– Ask what the problem was.
– Apologize and make an excuse.
– Check the name of the hotel. Ask what the problem was.
– Apologize and make an excuse.
– Make an offer (offer another course).
– End the call.

FILE 24

Unit 1 Requests Task, p9

1 You work for WPC. Your partner will phone you and ask to speak to the Marketing Manager. She is on holiday. Use this information to answer your partner's questions.

Name of Marketing Manager: Saskia Pui-Yung.
E-mail address: saskia@wpc.co.uk
Telephone: 00 44 216 8988

2 Call Mateo SA and ask to speak to the Sales Manager. If he/she's not there, ask for their name, phone number, and e-mail address. Make a note of the information your partner gives you.

FILE 25
Unit 5 Arrangements 7, p51

1 You are Ewart Carson. Call Chris Lekh to arrange his/her talk.

- Explain why you are calling.
- Suggest some dates and times on the schedule, which aren't already taken.
- Ask for the title of the talk.
- Confirm the details and write the information on the schedule on page 50.

2 You are Alex Godfrey. You have agreed to do a seminar. Ewart Carson calls you to arrange a time.

- You are going on a business trip to Japan for the last two weeks in March (from 20 March).
- You are working until 7.30 p.m. on Monday evenings in March.
- The title of your talk is 'Culture and Communication'.

FILE 26
Unit 3 Organizing an event 5, p35

It is 25 April. You work at Pulsar Laser. You receive a call from a potential customer. Take details of the caller and answer their questions using the information below.

> **Dimensions of the Laser Show:** 18 m by 25 m. It is 4 m high.
> **Dates?** Fully booked in May except May 12th, May 13th, and May 14th.
> **Number of people:** 20 people for each show.
> **Duration of show:** Each laser fight lasts 30 minutes.
> **Cost:** £150 per game.
> **Deposit:** 25% deposit and the balance 14 days before the date. Refund 50% if the event is cancelled because of rain.
> **Booking:** Confirm information and take a booking if possible.

FILE 27
Unit 3 Product details 5, p34

1 You are a distributor and want to sell Lichfield rucksacks in your region. Your partner works for Lichfield. Call them and ask for the information below. Ask about the Arran brand of rucksack.

	Arran 60+	Arran 85
Size		
Weight		
Colour		
Price		
Material		

2 You work for Lichfield. Your partner, who is a distributor, calls you and asks for information about the items below. Use the information to answer their questions.

Lichfield tents

	Inca 1800	Inca 2400
Size (packed)	23x80 cm	25x80 cm
Weight	6.8 kg	7.1 kg
No. of people	3	4
Price	€149	€189
Colour	Blue	Green

FILE 28
Unit 5 Making choices 10, p57

Your CEO is going to call you. He has a problem and wants to change next Thursday's meeting. You are busy all day Tuesday and Wednesday, and on Friday before 11.30 a.m.

FILE 29

Unit 3 Organizing an event Task, p35

You have got information about two places for your company's event. Call your partner and exchange information. Your partner has information about two other places. Ask your partner about them and make notes.

	Health club	Restaurant
Name	Spatown	La Table
No. of people	50	40
Distance from head office	500 km	2 km
Food	Vegetarian supper	French 3 courses
Drink	Free fruit juice	House wine $15 bottle
Opening hours	7–11 p.m.	8–11 p.m.
Cost per person	€35/person	€45/person
Special offers	Free massage and swimming	Free minibus service home

FILE 30

Unit 5 Arrangements 7, p51

1 You are Chris Lekh. You have agreed to do a seminar. Ewart Carson calls you to arrange a time.
- From 1 March to 14 March you are going on holiday.
- On 18 and 19 March you are attending a conference in Los Angeles.
- Title of your talk is 'Managing change'.

2 You are Ewart Carson. Call Alex Godfrey to arrange his/her talk.
- Explain why you are calling.
- Suggest some dates and times on the schedule, which aren't already taken.
- Ask for the title of the talk.
- Confirm the details and write the information on the schedule on page 50.

FILE 31

Unit 4 Checking facts 6, p43

1 You work at the Hotel Schuman. Use the information below when your partner calls you.
- 10 minutes from central station but 20 minutes from Eurostar station.
- Double room from €82 for bed & breakfast, does not include dinner.
- Restaurant closes at 11 p.m.
- Nearest metro is Schuman.
- Confirm price and dates.
- Your fax is: +32 (0)5453 157**7**.

2 Call the Hotel Soleil to check some information. Use the advertisement on page 42 to help you.
- Check number of stars.
- Five minutes from centre – by car or on foot?
- Check nearest metro is Metro Parc.
- Confirm price. You want a single room with shower.
- Check price includes breakfast.
- Confirm facts about restaurant.
- Check availability and book a room.
- Ask for fax number.

FILE 32

Unit 4 Solving a problem Task, p45

1 You are Nicholas Grand. Someone from the training company calls you to discuss your complaint. Answer their questions using your letter and the information below.
- You attended the course from 17–18 March.
- The name of your trainer was Tim Watts.
- You paid $450 for the course.
- Make a complaint about the course.
- Hotel was The Century Hotel – make a complaint about it.
- You want a refund not another course.
- You would like a written reply to your complaint.

FILE 33

Unit 4 Dealing with complaints Task, p39

1 You work for a cell phone company. Your partner is one of your customers. Call your partner to check that they are satisfied with your service. If they are dissatisfied offer them the special deals in the last column. Complete the form below.

CUSTOMER CARE **FRESH PHONES**

Name: .... Telephone number: 0778 456321

	Very satisfied	Satisfied	Dissatisfied	Action (if problem)
The telephone	☐	☐	☐	Give new model
Messaging service	☐	☐	☐	Give 3 months free
Network	☐	☐	☐	Give 5% off next bill
International use	☐	☐	☐	Give €10 free calls
Payment system	☐	☐	☐	Send bill showing cost for each call

Check your customer knows about these new services:

Travel news	YES ☐	NO ☐		Send information
Sports results	YES ☐	NO ☐		Send information

2 You had a two-week holiday in Florida recently. The holiday company calls you to check you were happy with everything. Use the information below to reply. Complain when necessary.

- The flight was 3 hours late.
- The JTC representative arrived 30 minutes late to meet you.
- The hotel wasn't very comfortable. You were very unhappy with it.
- The entertainment was very good.
- The food was fine but there was not always enough.
- JTC staff were very friendly.
- You haven't received the new JTC brochure yet.

FILE 34

Unit 3 Telephoning Task, p29

1 You work for ITC. Your partner will call you for more information. Use this information to answer their questions.

- Answer the phone and give your name.
- ITC offers up to 50% discount on 17,000 hotels. (It is often 20%.)
- ITC will find the lowest-priced flights.
- For more information – www.goitc.com

2 Call your partner and find out the following information about ITC. Check it carefully! Introduce yourself at the start of the call. Get the information and end the call politely.

- Introduce yourself.
- Discount on car rental? How much?
- How much to join?
- Travel insurance? How much for?

FILE 35

Unit 4 Checking facts 6, p43

1 Call the Hotel Schuman to check some information. Look at the advertisement on page 42 to help you.

- Confirm the distance from the station.
- What about the Eurostar station?
- You are interested in a double room. Check the price of the room includes breakfast and dinner.
- You are arriving at 10 p.m. Check restaurant times.
- Check nearest metro.
- Book room and check price and dates.
- Ask for fax number.

2 You work at the Hotel Soleil. Use the information below when your partner calls you.

- Family hotel 5 minutes by car from city centre.
- Metro Parc is the nearest metro.
- €65 single without shower. €70 with shower. €75 double with shower.
- Free breakfast.
- No restaurant at the hotel. Great choice of restaurant 5 minutes away.
- Confirm price and dates.
- Your fax number: +32 (0)5033 7855

FILE 36

Unit 4 Checking facts Task, p43

1 You left a message for your partner to call you. When your partner returns your call, use this information.

- Your name is Kate Hawkins.
- You attended a press conference last week (6th June) about a new hotel in Dubai.
- You are a journalist on the *Daily Post*.
- Your e-mail address is: KHawkins@aol.com.
- Your article will appear in next Sunday's newspaper (17 June).

2 Look at the notes you took below and check the information.

Royal Meridien Hotel Dubai
How many beds? 1,000?
Near Jumera (?) beach
Price per night $600 (?)
Large health club with five hammams (what?)
Rooms are cheaper in summer (why?)

FILE 37

Unit 1 Asking for information Task, p7

1 You are a receptionist at a hotel. Your partner is a guest. Look at this information and answer your partner's questions.

GUEST INFORMATION

Breakfast Breakfast is served 6.30 – 10.00 a.m. in the Blue Room (see plan below).

Lunch/Dinner Good food in our two restaurants (see plan).
Sammy's Salad Bar: 11.45 a.m. – 10.30 p.m.
El Pescador: 6.30 – 12.00 p.m.

Airport shuttle Free bus service to the international airport (20-minute journey). First bus at 7.15 a.m., then every half hour until 6.45 p.m.

Change There is no bureau de change in the hotel, but there is a bank just opposite the main entrance to the hotel. Open 8.15 a.m. – 4.30 p.m. Mon – Fri.

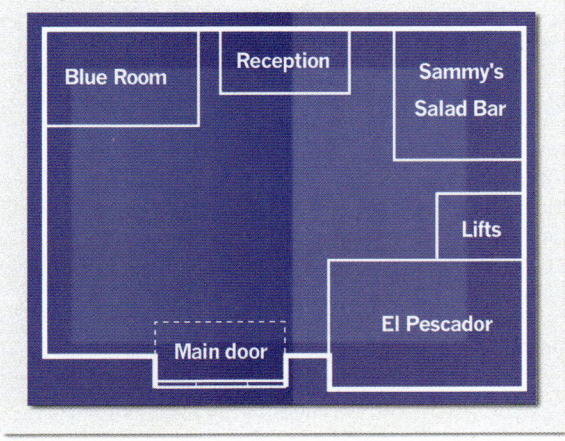

[Floor plan showing: Blue Room, Reception, Sammy's Salad Bar, Lifts, El Pescador, Main door]

2 You are a hotel guest and you want this information. Ask your partner questions.

- Where telephones? Credit card phones?
- Business centre with computers in hotel? Where? What time/open/close?
- Newspapers/hotel? What time/ arrive/morning?
- Good jazz clubs/near here? Where? Concert/this evening? What time/start?

FILE 38

Unit 3 Telephoning 3, p28

1 You receive a phone call from your partner. Use these notes to help you.

- Answer the phone and give your company name (SIO).
- Offer to help.
- Your fax number is 00 32 4202 36 37

2 Call your partner to get their company's website address.

- Introduce yourself.
- Say where you are calling from and why.
- Thank the person at the other end.

FILE 39

Unit 5 Ideas Task, p49

These are some ideas you have for promoting and advertising new Life Force sweets.

a advertise on TV – 20 commercials of 15 seconds over 6 weeks
   Cost: €8 million
b sponsor a big national marathon – advertisements at start/finish line
   Cost: €2.5 million
c do a mailshot – send 4 million letters to people in 16–40 age group
   Cost: €1.5 million
d offer free samples in shops – 16 days in 160 different pharmacies and sports shops
   Cost: € 0.5 million

1 Make your suggestions to your partner and listen to your partner's suggestions.

2 You have a total advertising budget for the year of €15 million. Decide which ideas to choose.

You can start like this:
How about advertising on TV? It would cost €8 million for 20 commercials of 15 seconds over 6 weeks.

Unit 1
Out and about

1.1

SL Hello. Can I introduce myself? I am Sylvie Leray. I work for Michelin, in Ladoux in France. I'm a research scientist.

PB Nice to meet you. My name's Pietro Benedetti. I'm from Bologna in Italy originally, but now I live in Torino. I'm an engineer at Fiat.

1.2

FI Hi. Can I introduce myself? I'm Fernanda Inez.

TS How do you do. My name's Tomas Sammler.

FI Nice to meet you. Are you German?

TS Yes, I am. And where do you come from, Fernanda?

FI Well, originally I'm from Portugal. But I work in Spain.

TS And who do you work for?

FI El Aguila.

TS What does your company do?

FI We're part of the Heineken group. We produce beer for the Spanish market. What about you?

TS I work for Bosch. We make parts for the car industry.

FI Oh really. And where are you based?

TS Well, my office is in Frankfurt, but I travel all over Europe. And where do you work?

FI In Madrid. But I travel a lot too.

1.3

a It's just here, in front of you, to the left of the departure gate.
b Yes, there is. It's over there on the right, just next to the main exit.
c It's just here on your right, opposite the departure gate.
d Yes, there are. There's one right next to the reservations desk on your right, and another one over there between the information desk and the first aid room.
e They're at the other end of the main concourse, on the left, near the restaurant. But there's also one over there, just next to the departure gate.

1.4

a A Excuse me. Where's the check-in area?
   B It's just here, in front of you, to the left of the departure gate.
b C Excuse me. Is there a toilet near here?
   D Yes, there is. It's over there on the right, just next to the main exit.
c E Excuse me. Where's the reservations desk?
   F It's just here on your right, opposite the departure gate.
d G Excuse me. Are there any car hire companies near here?
   H Yes, there are. There's one right next to the reservations desk on your right, and another one over there between the information desk and the first aid room.
e I Excuse me. Where are the lifts?
   J They're at the other end of the main concourse, on the left, near the restaurant. But there's also one over there, just next to the departure gate.

1.5

A Excuse me. What time does the plane from Glasgow arrive?
B From Glasgow? It arrives at … ten past two.

C Sorry to bother you. What time do the shops open here?
D They are open from six-thirty in the morning.
C And what time do they close?
D At quarter past ten in the evening. But on Sundays they close earlier, at nine-thirty.

E Excuse me, is there a flight to Frankfurt this afternoon?
F Yes, there's just one flight.
E What time does it leave?
F At twenty-five to one.
E Sorry, twelve thirty-five?
F Yes, that's right.

G Excuse me, is there a bureau de change here?
H Yes, it's open from nine in the morning until eleven-thirty at night.
G Eleven-thirty. OK, thanks.

1.6

So, if you would like more information about 'smile', call them on oh one six one four double seven one nine two seven. That's zero one six one four double seven one nine two seven, or send an e-mail to enquiry at smile dot co dot U-K. That's enquiry at smile dot co dot U-K. Or visit the website at W-W-W dot smile dot co dot U-K forward slash demo.

1.7

A Hello, Jules Verne Publishing.
B Hello. Can I speak to Alex Fielding, please?
A I'm afraid he's not here this afternoon.
B Could you ask him to call me back tomorrow or he can e-mail me?
A Certainly. Can you tell me your name, please?
B Yes, it's Philip Carter, C-A-R-T-E-R. I'm Regional Sales Manager of Cista Systems. That's C-I-S-T-A Systems.
A Cista Systems, OK. Could I have your phone number?
B Yes, it's a cell phone number. It's 0776 332 5498.
A 0776 332 5498. OK. And can I take your e-mail address too?
B Sure, it's p dot carter at c-i-double s-y-s dot com.
A OK, Mr Carter. I'll give him the message.

B Thanks for your help. Goodbye.
A Goodbye.

1.8

EM Stefan, hello. Nice to see you again.
ST It's nice to be here, Elena. How are you?
EM I'm fine. And you?
ST I'm very well, thank you.
EM That's good. I'm sorry I'm late – the traffic is very bad today.
ST No problem. I'm free all day.
EM I'm glad to hear that. Oh, I'm afraid Oscar is ill today – he can't come to the meeting.
ST Oh, I'm sorry to hear that.
EM Yes, it is a pity. OK, let's go to my office … (*pause*) OK, Stefan. Please come in and have a seat.
ST Thanks. Can I plug in my laptop somewhere?
EM Of course. Go ahead. There's a socket over there.
ST Thank you.
EM You're welcome.

1.9

EM So, would you like a coffee before we start?
ST No, thanks, I'm fine.
EM OK. Would you like to meet the other people on the team?
ST Yes, please. But could we do it later?
EM Yes, of course.
ST I need to make a couple of calls, you see.
EM OK. Would you like to use my phone?
ST Thank you, that's very kind of you.
EM No problem. Would you like a message pad to take notes?
ST No, thanks. I've some paper here.

1.10

A Let's go to my office. It's this way
B OK, after you. (*pause*)
A Right. (*pause*) Here we are …
B Thank you. Mmm, what a lovely office!
A Yes, it is. Please come in.
B Thank you.
A Have a seat.
B Thanks very much.

A Would you like a coffee?
B Yes, please. That would be nice.
A OK, just one second. Here you are.
B Thanks very much.
A You're welcome.

1.11

A So, first can I introduce you to Tom Saverys, our Business Development Manager.
B Hello.
A And this is my Personal Assistant, Petra Mantegazza.
C Hello.
A OK. So this is the organization chart of Soft Plan.
D OK.
A As you can see, four managers report directly to me. That's the Quality Manager, the Operations Manager, the Accounts Manager, and the Business Development Manager.
D And I see that the Sales Manager reports to the Business Development Manager.
A Yes, that's right. Tom is in charge of finding new markets for our products, and the Sales Manager is responsible for optimizing sales in those markets.
D OK, that's clear.
A Then three people report to the Operations Manager. First, there are the two Chief Engineers. They manage the Electrical Design and Software Development teams.
D How many people are there in the teams?
A Ten people in Electrical Design and fifteen in Software.
D OK.
A Then finally there's the Production Manager, who manages the factory.
D I see.

1.12

1 A Excuse me. Is there a bank near here?
B Yes, there is, sir. There's a Chinese restaurant opposite the hotel, and the bank is next to the restaurant, on the right.
A Great. And what time does it open?
B At a quarter to nine, I think.

2 C Could we have a table next to a window, please?
D Yes, of course. There's one over there. Can I take your coats?
E Yes. Thanks.
D Would you like to come this way? … Here you are. Would you like a drink before your meal?
C Yes, please. Could you bring us a bottle of champagne, please?
D Yes, of course, Madam.

3 F Can I introduce you to my colleague, Guler Marlet?
G How do you do?
H Pleased to meet you.
F Guler is responsible for European sales. She reports directly to our Sales Director in London.
G Sorry, I didn't catch your first name?
H It's Guler. That's G-U-L-E-R.
G And where are you from, Guler?
H From Turkey originally. But now I live in Paris.

4 (*one side of telephone call*)
Could I speak to Alex Ling, please? (…) No, thanks. That's not necessary. Could you ask him to call me back tomorrow, please? (…) Yes, it's a cell phone number. It's 08 41 32 77 96. (…) Yes, it's Paula Broadbent, that's B-R-O-A-D-B-E-N-T. (…) Great. Thanks for your help. (…) Goodbye.

1.13

A Could I speak to Alex Ling, please?
B I'm afraid he's not here. Would you like to speak to his assistant?
A No, thanks. That's not necessary. Could you ask him to call me back tomorrow, please?
B Yes, of course. Could I have your number, please?
A Yes, it's a cell phone number. It's 08 41 32 77 96.
B OK. I've got that. And could you give me your name, please?
A Yes, it's Paula Broadbent, that's B-R-O-A-D-B-E-N-T.
B Right, Mrs Broadbent. I'll give him your message.
A Great. Thanks for your help.
B You're welcome.
A Goodbye.

Unit 2
Presenting your company

2.1
a McDonald's sells fast food all over the world.
b General Motors manufactures cars and other vehicles.
c Thomas Cook Travel organizes package holidays.
d Cellnet operates cell phone networks.
e Sekisui House constructs luxury homes.
f Banco Bradesco provides banking services.
g AOL Time Warner publishes *Time* and *Fortune* magazines.
h IBM produces software solutions.

2.2
1 A And what does your company do?
   B We build high-quality houses all over Japan. We also construct restaurants and hotels, and manage other big construction projects.
   A Do you have any other activities?
   B Yes, we now also produce computer software and information systems.
2 A Your company's American, isn't it?
   B Yes, it is. But we manufacture cars all over the world. Other companies in the group include Opel and Vauxhall. We also work with Suzuki and Fiat.
   A Do you only make cars?
   B No, we produce trucks too.
3 A Where does your company operate?
   B Well, mostly in our country. We have 2,400 branches in Brazil, where we provide a range of financial and banking services.
   A And what other services do you provide?
   B Well, we sell insurance, and then we also offer free Internet banking to our customers. Oh yes, and we can also provide credit cards in the colours of our customers' favourite Brazilian football team.
   A Really!

2.3
A So, what does SF do?
B We manufacture and supply parts to the aeronautical industry and we maintain aircraft.
A And where are you based?
B Well we are actually part of the Ruag Suisse Group and our head office is in Emmen in Switzerland.

2.4
A How many people do you employ?
B In total there are about 1,600 employees.
A Who are your main customers?
B Well, three of our biggest customers are British Aerospace, Dasa, and Boeing.
A And how many sites do you have?
B The company has seven sites in Switzerland with a total factory area of 77,000 m².
A Wow, that's quite a lot. And how much office space do you have?
B The office area is about 19,000 m².
A So, how much money does SF make per year?
B Well, our annual turnover is currently about 400,000,000 Swiss francs.

2.5
1 S Hello John, this is Sarah in reception. Could I have some help, please?
   J Sorry Sarah. We're all in a meeting. We're preparing a new advertising campaign.
   S OK. Thanks anyway.
2 A Hello, Angus speaking.
   S Hi Angus. This is Sarah. The phone hasn't stopped ringing this morning and so I can't speak to visitors. Could you ask someone to come and help me for a while?
   A I'm afraid we're all busy Sarah. It's the end of the month and we're doing our monthly figures for the bank.
   S Oh, OK.
3 S Hi Fiona, this is Sarah in reception. Are you busy?
   F Yes. I'm interviewing candidates for the new job. Sorry, I must go.
   S OK. Thanks for your help.

2.6
A So, why are you travelling round Spain?
B We are developing a new product for the Spanish market, so I'm visiting customers here to find out what they want. What about you? What are you doing here?
A We're working on a project with a Spanish company. We're looking at ways to promote business travel in this area. Where are you staying?
B At the Hilton. And you?
A Oh, I'm staying with some friends who live in Bilbao.

2.7
Aristotle Onassis was born in Turkey in 1906. His father Socrates was a rich man. Onassis moved to Argentina in 1923 and started working for a telephone company. He saved a lot of money and started his own export business. In 1946 he bought his first oil tanker and in 1953 he founded a new shipping company in Monte Carlo called Olympic Maritime. This was the holding company for all his business activities. In 1963 he returned close to home and bought the Greek island of Skorpios. Five years later in 1968 he married the widow of John Kennedy, Jackie. He died in Paris in 1975.

2.8
OK. This is a very popular product. It's sold in restaurants and supermarkets.

It's made all over the world, but originally it comes from Italy. It's usually packed in a box, a cardboard box. The product is often bought by people who don't have much time. It's sometimes delivered to their home or office by motorcycle.

2.9
We have four springs in the US. The spring for this plant is in Pennsylvania.

First, the water is taken from the spring. Special stainless steel trucks are then used to transport the water to the plant. Every year about 750 million litres of water are delivered to the plant. So how is it treated? First, it is filtered to remove sand and things like that. Then it is disinfected to remove bacteria. After that it is checked in our laboratory for purity and then bottled. The bottles are then packed. Finally they are transported by road or rail to the stores.

2.10

The head office and main factory of BASF are in Ludwigshafen in Germany, but we are a truly global company. We have 133 subsidiaries worldwide, with production sites in 38 different countries, and customers in more than 170. To meet the needs of those customers, we have a total of around 100,000 employees. More than half of these are in Germany – about 55,000. In Asia and the Far East, we have about 10,000 employees. And in Latin America the figure is about 7,000.

Our worldwide turnover last year was 35.9 billion euros, and we invested 1.5 billion of this in research.

2.11

We are currently working on a number of new projects. Firstly, construction. We are building a number of new chemical production plants at the moment with our local partners in China and Malaysia.

The second area is plant science. We are doing research into plant biotechnology in a number of sites, in Germany, Sweden, the United States, and Canada. We're working with a Swedish company, Svalöf Weibull.

Then there's the area of plastics production. Our partner in this new joint venture is the Shell company. Together we are manufacturing the plastics polyethylene and polypropylene.

2.12

When Friedrich Engelhorn founded our company in 1865, we produced industrial dyes.

In the 1920s we invested a lot of money in fuels and synthetic rubber because of the rapid development of the motor car.

In 1925, economic conditions were very bad. BASF merged with several other companies, and the headquarters moved to Frankfurt.

BASF researchers are famous for their inventions. In 1951 our scientists created 'Styropor', a product still used today for food packaging and insulation in houses.

The 1960s marked the beginning of our global expansion. We constructed new plants in Europe, North and South America, and the Far East. After 1965 we added many new product lines, including drugs and agricultural chemicals. The 1980s and 1990s were a period of investment in Asia and the Far East, first in South Korea, then in China.

Unit 3
Exchanging information

3.1

A Good morning. Veronafiere. Danilo Riazzo speaking. How can I help?
B Hello, this is Alan O'Brien. I'm calling from Ireland. I work for a whisky manufacturer. I understand you organize trade fairs and exhibitions. Could you give me some information, please?

3.2

B Could you give me some information, please?
A Certainly. What would you like to know?
B Do you have an exhibition for the drinks business?
A Yes we do. It's called Vinitaly.
B Sorry. Could you say that again, please?
A VINITALY. We hold it in the spring every year. This year it's April 11th–15th.
B Mmm. Do you get many visitors?
A Last year we had nearly 135,000 visitors.
B Italian visitors I presume.
A Mainly, but we did have about 15,000 foreign visitors.
B Sorry, did you say fifty thousand?
A No fifteen. One five.
B That's very interesting. What were the dates again?
A The 11th April to 15th April.
B Could you send me some information?
A All the information is available on our website at veronafiere.co.it.
B Great, I'll have a look. Sorry, was that dot net or dot I-T?
A Dot I-T.
B Ah right. OK Thanks for your help.
A Oh, you're welcome. Thanks for calling. Bye.

3.3

A So, what's your job like, Claudia?
B It's fine but the hours are very long. What about you, Karl?
A Well my day is quite short, but I live about eighty kilometres away, so I have to travel three hours every day.
B Wow, I'm quite lucky then. I live about two minutes away, so I can go home for lunch!
A I can't do that. I have to eat in our canteen but the food is very good … and it's cheap!
B What time do you finish work?
A Usually about 4.30. What about you?
B Well, I often have to work quite late. My boss is in the US and he often calls me late afternoon to ask me to do something for him.
A Mm, I'm really lucky – I never have to work late. But can you start work a bit later then?
B No, everyone has to be at the office by 9.00 a.m.
A We can choose the hours we want to work.
B That's really good. Well, at least I get plenty of holiday. We get thirty days a year. What about you?
A We have twenty-five days a year. We usually go to Spain for a month, in August.

B Lucky you! We can't take holidays in July or August and we can only take two weeks at one time …

3.4

T Sally. How are you? How is New York?
S Great. I love my new job.
T What are you doing?
S I work for a magazine.
T Good salary?
S Not bad. It's higher than Paris but lower than London. What about you? Are you still in Paris?
T No, I moved to London last year. I work for the same company but I'm at the Head Office.
S How do you find England?
T Very expensive. My rent is higher than it was in Paris and food is much more expensive.
S Of the three I think New York is the cheapest for food. What about tax?
T I pay about 30% in London. In Paris I paid about 35%. What do you pay in New York?
S About 40% altogether. So, what about holidays?
T They are longer in France. I had six weeks per year. Here I get four!
S You're lucky. In New York I only get two weeks a year!

3.5

A Hello. I'm calling to order some sleeping bags for our mountaineering club. Do you have any in stock?
B Yes we do. The Cyclone is an excellent sleeping bag.
A OK. How long is it?
B It's 1 m 90.
A And the width?
B 75 cm. It's fine for an adult.
A What size is it when it's packed?
B 17 by 30 so quite small.
A OK. How heavy is it?
B It weighs 1 kg.
A And what colour is it?
B It's red on the outside and yellow inside.
A And one more question. How much is it?
B $25.
A OK. Do you have six in stock?
B I'll just check …

3.6

J Hello, is that Pulsar Laser?
M Yes. My name is Maria. How can I help?
J My name is James Robertson. I'm calling from Manchester. Are you still taking bookings for May?
M Yes, we are.
J How big is the equipment?
M The tent, you mean?
J Yeah.
M Well, it's a large tent about 20 m by 15 m.
J Sorry, did you say 20 by 50?
M No, 20 by 15.
J OK, and how much does it cost for a half day?
M £600. That time includes putting the tent up.
J And how long does a game usually last?
M About 30 minutes.
J Good. Are you free on May 12th?
M Let me check. Sorry, did you say the 12th?
J Yes, that's right.
M Yes, we are free at the moment.
J Could I think about it for a bit?
M Certainly. No problem. Thanks for your call.

Unit 4
Getting things done

4.1

N OK, Charlie. Can we have a look at the list of things that Diane left for you to do while she's away?
C Sure.
N Right. Have you arranged the trip to Milan, yet?
C Yes, I have. I've booked the plane and the hotel.
N Excellent. Now, what about the press conference? Have you sent the invitations out?
C No, not yet. I'm just doing the envelopes now.
N OK. That's good. They really need to be sent out as soon as possible. And have you had a chance to call the electrician?
C Yes, I called him this morning and he came immediately and fixed the lights.
N That's good news! And what about the stationery? Have you ordered it yet?
C Yes, I sent the order on Tuesday.
N Great. Just one more thing. Have you done the minutes of the marketing meeting?
C No, I'm afraid I haven't had time, but I'll do them this afternoon.
N Good. Could you e-mail me a copy, please?
C Sure.

4.2

1 A AJB, how can I help you?
  B Good morning. I placed an order with your company five weeks ago and I haven't received any goods yet!
  A I'm very sorry. It's because we are still waiting for new stock.
  B Oh, I see.
  A Right. Could I have your order number? I'll just check your order.
  B Thanks very much. It's 3564ST.
2 C Excuse me?
  D Yes?
  C My room's really cold.
  D I'm sorry about that. I'm afraid we switched off all the heating last weekend. I'll send a technician to switch it on again.
  C Don't worry. I'm checking out at midday.
3 F Excuse me?
  E Yes?
  F It's very noisy.
  E Yes, I'm sorry, sir. It's because we have a school party on the flight.
  F I can see that.
  E I'll see if there's a seat free in business class.
  F No, it's OK. But can I have another drink?
  E Certainly, sir.

4.3

A OK. Next item on the agenda is the Paris project. There is a lot to do. Have we contacted any estate agents?
B Not yet. Shall I do that?
A Yes, please. We need a list of four or five places to visit.

C I appointed an architect last week so he can visit the premises with us.
A OK. So first we need to find the premises. Then we should get planning permission if necessary, then organize the building work. Carla? Could you do all that with the architect?
C Certainly.
B When we are sure about the building, I'll order the furniture and recruit the staff. We need at least three people. I'll advertise in the *Herald Tribune*.
C We should install the telephones and computers right at the end. Two weeks before opening so we have time to check everything.
A Shall I do that?
B Could you? And I'll organize some advertising and PR events two months before we open. Shall I organize the launch party at the same time?
A Yes, OK.

4.4

A Hello, I saw your advertisement in *Metro* magazine and I'd just like to check some details about your hotel.
B Certainly, sir.
A OK. Your ad says you're eight minutes from the city centre. Is that right?
B Yeah, that's right.
A Is that by metro or on foot?
B On foot.
A Great, and can I just check that your restaurant's open late at night?
B Yes, that's right. Until 1 a.m.
A … and you serve vegetarian food?
B Yes, we do.
A I suppose the nearest metro is Maclou?
B No, in fact it's Louisa.
A Perfect. Could I book a double room for this weekend?
B Just a moment, please. Yes, that's fine. Arriving Friday 23rd?
A Yes, and leaving on Sunday 25th. The second night is free, right?
B No, it's actually the third night that's free.
A Oh, I see.

B Would you like to stay on Sunday night as well, then?
A Mm, yes, please. So we'll leave on Monday the 26th. Could you just confirm the price for two, please?
B €80 per night for two people. That makes a total of €160 for the three nights.
A That's excellent. Shall I send you a fax to confirm my reservation?
B Yes, please.
A And your fax number is 32 02513 9103, is that right?
B Yes, that's it.

4.5

a Hello. This is Nicholas Grand. I wrote to you last week and I haven't had a reply yet. Please call me on 01865 407555. Thank you.
b Good morning Peter. This is Charlotte. I hope all is well. Listen I have paid the March salaries and I organized the mailshot before I left so you can cross them off the list. Bye.
c Hello, this is Mr Larsen. Please reply to my e-mail as quickly as possible. We would like to arrange the course for the third week of April.
d Good morning. This is Mr Platt from the bank. Your overdraft has increased to $750. Could you call to arrange an appointment.

Unit 5
Planning ahead

5.1

A What do you think of the proposal for the on-line catalogue?
B I think it's a great idea. It'll reduce our advertising costs. In the future we won't have to send a catalogue to every customer. What do you think?
A I don't know. I don't think it'll work.
B Why not?
A Because a lot of our customers won't like it. It's very quick and easy to look in a printed catalogue, but the Internet is often very slow.
B I disagree. I think it'll save time for our customers. They often order the

same things. On the Internet our customers will just press a button to repeat their order. It'll be very quick.
A OK, maybe that's true, but it won't be cheap. It'll cost a lot of money to develop this website.
B Well, not really. I have the figures here. Have a look …
A Mmm …
B And of course, customers will be able to buy our latest products because we'll be able to update the catalogue regularly.
A That's a good point.

5.2

A So, we've got some really good beers. A lot of pubs and bars are interested. But now we need to promote them to the public. Any ideas?
B How about going to bars in the evening and giving customers free tastings?
A Yes, that's not a bad idea. And in supermarkets too. But there is another possibility. Why don't we offer free tours of the brewery?
B Well, I'm not really sure about that. If we want people to come to the brewery, we'll need to advertise in the press. That's very expensive.
A Well, maybe not. We could contact the local radio station – they often organize competitions for their listeners. You know, 'answer these three questions correctly …'
B '… and you can win a free visit to a local brewery'?
A Yes, exactly.
B Christopher, that's a great idea.

5.3

A … So, the talks are in March. There are a number of possible dates. When are you free, Simon?
B Let me check in my diary. The second week would be good – that's the week of the 9th to the 13th.
A Are you free on Friday 13th?
B Is that for a talk in the evening?
A Yes, they're all in the evening.
B Oh, I'm sorry, but I'm going away that weekend.

How about Thursday of that week?
A No, I'm afraid someone else is speaking on that day.
B Oh dear.
A What are you doing later in the month? Are you free on the 25th or the 27th?
B Let me see. Yes, Friday the 27th is fine.
A Great. Is six o'clock OK?
B Well, I'd prefer a little later if possible.
A Well, people don't like to stay late on a Friday evening.
B OK, then six o' clock is fine.
A Thanks very much Simon. So that's Friday the 27th at six, then. Oh, one more thing. Do you have a title for your talk?
B Yes, it's 'Management Meetings: Small is Beautiful'.
A Great. Thanks very much Simon.

5.4
A Well, it was a very interesting morning. Thank you for inviting me.
B You're welcome.
A It was nice to meet everybody.
B I'm glad you enjoyed it. So, have a nice afternoon at the Coliseum.
A Thank you very much.
B And see you at your hotel at 7 o'clock.
A Yes, see you later.

5.5
a A Thank you very much for coming to see us.
  B Thank you for inviting me.
b A It was a very interesting visit.
  B And you.
c A See you again next month.
  B Yes. I look forward to it.
d A It was very nice to see you again.
  B Yes, I hope so.
e A Have a good week.
  B I'm glad you enjoyed it.
f A And thanks for helping me with my presentation.
  B It was a pleasure.
g A See you next year, maybe.
  B Yes, I hope so.
h A Have a good trip back.
  B Thanks. You too.

5.6
a Thank you very much for coming to see us.
b It was a very interesting visit.
c See you again next month.
d It was very nice to see you again.
e Have a good week.
f And thanks for helping me with my presentation.
g See you next year, maybe.
h Have a good trip back.

5.7
A OK, can we start? As you know, we plan to close our Manchester office in December. There are fifty employees working there in Customer Service. We hope to move the Customer Service Department to London in August.
B Fifty people! But we don't have enough office space in London.
A At present, no. We'll need to find about another 200 m² of office space before the summer.
C How are we going to do that?
A We're going to reduce the number of people that use the London offices. We're here today to discuss how we can do that.

5.8
A Can I have your ideas, then?
C How about making our offices open-plan? I'm sure we can save a lot of space like that.
A Well, I'm not sure about that. It'll be very expensive to make all those changes.
B Yes, I agree. And I don't think managers will want to lose their individual offices.
C So, do you have a better suggestion?
B Yes, why don't we ask some employees to work from home?
A Teleworking, you mean?
B Yes.
A That's not a bad idea.
C Well, personally, I don't think it'll work. There'll be a problem of productivity, I'm sure. People work harder in the office than they do at home.
A I've got another idea. We could ask our sales staff to share offices. They don't need a permanent office because they're out visiting clients for most of the week.
B Well, I think that'll cause problems. The sales staff are usually here on a Monday or Friday. They'll all want an office or desk at the same time.
C Yes, that's true.

5.9
A So, can you think about all this? And then we'll meet again next week to discuss it. When are you free?
B How about Tuesday afternoon?
C No, I'm sorry, but I'm going to Munich that day. I'd prefer the end of the week, if possible.
A Are you free on Thursday morning?
C Yes, that's fine.
B Yes, OK.
A Say 9.30?
B Fine.
C Sure.
A Great. Thank you for coming today. It was a very useful meeting.
C Yes, it was.
B Have a good weekend then, and see you next Thursday at 9.30.
C OK.
A Fine.

Glossary

the **accounts** a record of the money a company makes and spends

an **advertisement** information in newspapers and magazines, on television, etc. that tries to sell a product or service. Also *an advertising campaign, to advertise, an ad*

to **apologize** to say sorry. Also *to make an apology*

an **appointment** a meeting at an agreed time and place, usually with just one person

to **arrange** to plan a time for a meeting, conference, etc.

to **attend** to be present at a meeting, conference, etc.

to be **available** (of a person) free to do something; (of an object) free to be used immediately

average describes the usual or middle number in a group of numbers, e.g. *What's the average salary in your country?*; *The average of 1, 5, and 6 is 4.*

the **balance** the difference between the first payment(s) for a product or service and the total cost

to be **based** where a company (or person) has its main office, e.g. *We're based in London.*

a **bill** the document which shows the price to pay in a restaurant, hotel, etc.

the **Board** the people who control a company.

to **book** to reserve (a hotel room, flight, etc.). Also *to make a booking*

a **brochure** a thin book with illustrations that advertises a company and its products

a **budget** the amount of money you plan to spend on something

to be **busy** not free (for a person or telephone line)

to **call back** to phone somebody who has just phoned you

to **cancel** to say that something you have arranged won't happen. Also *to make a cancellation*

a **catalogue** a book which shows all of a company's products

a **cell phone** a telephone with no fixed line that you can use in the street, in different buildings, etc. Also called a *mobile* (UK) and a *cellular* (US)

to **charge** to ask for an amount of money for a service, e.g. *We charge $15 for delivery.*

a **check-in desk** the place where you register at a hotel, airport, etc. Also *to check in*

comfortable something that is easy and gives pleasure, not causing physical difficulties, e.g. *comfortable chairs/shoes*, etc.

a **commercial** see *advertisement*

common happening often, e.g. *a common mistake, problem,* etc.

a **competition** a game to win a prize. Also *the competition* or *competitors* – other companies that sell the same products as you

to **complain** to say that you are not happy about something. Also *to make a complaint*

a **conference** a special meeting where a lot of people discuss their work or interests

to **confirm** to say the details of a meeting, reservation, order, etc. to make sure they are final. Also *a confirmation*

consumer goods products that are sold to people not to companies

to **create** to make something new, e.g. *to create a company or a new product*

a **customer** someone who buys products and services

a **database** an organized list of information (names, addresses, etc.) on a computer

a **deadline** the date when something must be finished

a **deal** a commercial offer or promotion, e.g. *We have a special deal this month – 25% off all furniture.*

to **deal** with something to do something about solving a problem, completing a task, etc.

a **dealer** a person or company that sells a particular product, e.g. cars

a **defect** something wrong with a product, e.g. *There is a defect in this computer programme.*

to **deliver** to take or transport something to a particular place

a **department** a part of a company which has a particular function, e.g. *the Sales/Finance Department*

a **deposit** an initial payment for a product or service, e.g. *We ask for a 20% deposit when you order.*

to **design** to draw plans for something, e.g. *to design a house/clothes,* etc. Also *a designer*

to **develop** to change something to make it better, e.g. *We are developing a new model of this car.*

a **discount** an amount of money that is taken off the usual price, e.g. *We can offer a discount of 15%.*

an **employee** someone who works for a company. Also *to employ*, e.g. *The company employs 200 people.*

entertainment free-time activities: theatre shows, films, TV programmes, etc.

equipment machines or objects you need for a particular purpose, e.g. *audio-visual equipment*

an **exhibition** a public show of industrial products, works of art, etc.

experience knowledge obtained by practice of an activity, e.g. *He has experience in the computer industry.*

an **experiment** an action you take to try or test something for the first time

to **export** to send goods to another country for sale

facilities rooms, equipment, or services, e.g. *office facilities*

a **factory** a building with machines where goods are made

figures numbers in a table, graph, etc.

filing the process of organizing papers and documents so they are easy to find

to **found** to create (a company)

free not busy, e.g. *I'm free this afternoon for a meeting.*; at no cost, e.g. *The visit is €7 for adults, but free for children.*

to **give someone a hand** to offer someone your help

a **guest** someone you have invited to your house, company, etc., or a person staying in a hotel

a **head office** the main office of a company. Also *headquarters*

a **host** someone who receives a visitor

to **improve** to make something better

to **increase** to go up, e.g. *The number of accidents increased from 200 to 215.*

insurance a system of paying regular amounts in return for a bigger amount if you die, have an accident, etc., e.g. *life/house/car insurance*

to **interview** to ask someone questions (for a job, radio, or TV interview, etc.). Also *an interview*

to **invest** to spend money in order to make a profit, e.g. *to invest in the stock market*

to **invite** to ask someone to come somewhere or to do something

an **invoice** a document, usually between two companies, showing the goods sold and the price to be paid

an **item** one in a list of things, e.g. *an item on an order/invoice*

to **join** to start working for a company

a **laptop** a small computer which you can carry with you when you travel

to **last** to continue for a particular time, e.g. *The film lasts 98 minutes.*

to **launch** to show something, e.g. a product, to the public for the first time

a **mailshot** information sent to a large number of people at the same time

to **manufacture** to make things in large quantities using machines

a **market** a geographical area or a section of the population where you can sell products

to **merge** to join (with another company or other companies)

minutes a written report of what people said in a meeting

to **move** to change your house, business address, company, etc., e.g. *He moved to London last year.*

an **objective** the result you want a particular action to have, e.g. *The objective of this meeting is to choose a new product.*

to **operate** to do business in a particular place, e.g. *The company operates in all five continents.*

to **order** to ask formally for goods, e.g. *to order a new machine, a meal in a restaurant*, etc. Also *an order*, e.g. *to place an order*

an **organization chart** a diagram which shows the structure of a company

to **pack** to put goods in boxes, envelopes, etc. before sending them to customers

to **plug in** to connect an electrical machine or device

a **presentation** an organized talk about a subject, usually with visual information

a **press conference** a special meeting to give information (about your company, products, etc.) to the newspapers

a **press release** an article about your company sent to the newspapers

to **produce** to make something (to sell later), e.g. *We produce parts for cars.*

productivity the relation between speed and quantity of work done

a **project** a plan

to **provide** to give, to offer, e.g. *A bank provides financial services.*

a **quotation** a statement or estimate of the cost of a product or service

a **range** a group of products or services of the same type

a **receipt** a piece of paper which shows that you have paid for something

to **recruit** to find new employees for a company

to **reduce** to make smaller/less

a **refund** money paid back to you when you return goods that you do not want

to **remove** to take something from its place, e.g. *If you park there, the police will probably remove your car.*

to **rent** to pay money for the use of something, e.g. *to rent an office, a car*, etc. Also *a rental*

a **rep** someone who sells something for a company. Also *a sales rep, a sales representative*

a **report** a written (or spoken) description of an event, results of a study, etc.

a **request** something you ask for, e.g. *a request for information*

to **research** to find information in order to do a study of something, e.g. *We are researching new products.*

a **reservation** to ask in advance for a hotel room, travel ticket, etc.

revenue money from the sales of something

a **salary** the money you receive from a company for doing your job

a **sample** a product that you give free to customers to try before deciding to buy it

to **save** to keep money, usually in a bank, in order to buy something later

a **schedule** a plan of work, of a visit, etc., with times and dates

to **share** to use the same place, objects, etc. as other people, e.g. *to share work/an office/a computer*, etc.

single for one person, e.g. *a single room*

a **site** a place where a company has a factory/offices, etc.

software programmes for computers

to **solve** to find an answer to a problem

to **sort** to put things in groups

to **sponsor** to give money to an organization, etc., that agrees to advertise your company or its products

staff all the people who work for a company

a **stand** a small area at a trade fair or exhibition occupied by a company

stationery writing materials (pens, papers, etc.)

stock goods that have been made and are ready to sell, e.g. *We have 14 machines in stock.*

a **subsidiary** a company that is part of a bigger organization

to **supervise** to watch and be responsible for the work of people in a company

a **supplier** a company which sells goods to another company

to **switch on/off** to make a (usually electrical) machine start/stop working e.g. *to switch a computer on/off*

a **target** the results you want to obtain, usually expressed as a number, e.g. *Our sales target is 25,000 units for this year.*

a **task** a particular piece of work/something you need to do

a **tour** a guided visit

a **trade fair** an event where companies (usually in the same industry) show their products

to **train** to teach new skills (for work), e.g. *We're training people how to use the new programmes.*

a **trip** travel from one place to another, usually including the return

a **turnover** the value of a company's sales in dollars/euros, etc.

to **update** to add the most recent information

a **venue** the place where an event happens

voicemail an answering system in a company which gives information, transfers calls and records messages from callers

wealthy rich

a **website** pages on the Internet which give information about a company, institution, etc.

OXFORD
UNIVERSITY PRESS

Great Clarendon Street, Oxford OX2 6DP

Oxford University Press is a department of the University of Oxford. It furthers the University's objective of excellence in research, scholarship, and education by publishing worldwide in

Oxford New York

Auckland Bangkok Buenos Aires Cape Town Chennai Dar es Salaam Delhi Hong Kong Istanbul Karachi Kolkata Kuala Lumpur Madrid Melbourne Mexico City Mumbai Nairobi São Paulo Shanghai Singapore Taipei Tokyo Toronto

with an associated company in Berlin

Oxford and Oxford English are registered trade marks of Oxford University Press in the UK and in certain other countries

© Oxford University Press 2002

The moral rights of the author have been asserted

Database right Oxford University Press (maker)

First published 2002

No unauthorized photocopying

All rights reserved. No part of this publication may be reproduced, stored in a retrieval system, or transmitted, in any form or by any means, without the prior permission in writing of Oxford University Press, or as expressly permitted by law, or under terms agreed with the appropriate reprographics rights organization. Enquiries concerning reproduction outside the scope of the above should be sent to the ELT Rights Department, Oxford University Press, at the address above

You must not circulate this book in any other binding or cover and you must impose this same condition on any acquirer

Any websites referred to in this publication are in the public domain and their addresses are provided by Oxford University Press for information only. Oxford University Press disclaims any responsibility for the content.

ISBN 0 19 457288 9

Printed in Hong Kong

Acknowledgements

The authors and publisher are grateful to those who have given permission to reproduce the following extracts and adaptations of copyright material:

p 8 Information about Smile, The Internet Bank. Reproduced by permission of Smile.
p 17 Information about General Motors. Reproduced by permission of General Motors Corporation.
p 22 'Less stress, less money, more life' by Jonathon Savill. Appeared in Business Life October 2000. Reproduced by permission of Jonathon Savill
pp 61–2 Information about Liz Claiborne. Reproduced by permission of Liz Claiborne.
pp 26–7 Information about BASF from www.basf.de 2001. Reproduced by permission of BASF.
p 28 Information about Veronafiere from www.veronafiere.it. Reproduced by permission of Veronafiere.
pp 34, 60, 65 Information about Lichfield Products. Reproduced by permission of AMG Outdoor Ltd.
p 35 Information about Pulsar Mobile Laser Games. Reproduced by permission of Mark Burghard, owner.
p 48 Information about Christopher Bartlett, owner of Brasserie de la Soif. Reproduced by permission of Christopher Bartlett.
p 52 'Aston Martin revs up to roar towards profit' by David Parsley, © Times Newspapers Ltd 19 November 1999. Reproduced by permission.

Sources:
p 63 www.ericsson.se
p 59 www.toshiba.co.jp
p 59 www.bang-olufsen.com
p 63 www.samsungcorp.com
p 17 www.fortune.com (Sekisui House & Banco Bradesco)
p 18 SF Annual report 1999
p 19 www.cogema.fr
p 19 Sunday Telegraph 26/11/00 (Domino)

Illustrations by:
Mark Duffin pp 42, 59, 59
Tim Kahane pp 6, 7, 14, 25, 49, 57
Nigel Paige pp 9, 11, 20, 36, 38, 56

Commissioned photos by:
David Tolley pp 14 (restaurant), 46, 54.

The publisher would like to thank the following for their permission to reproduce photographs and other copyright material:

Airbus p 17; AMG Outdoor Ltd p 34 (objects); BASF p 26; British Telecom p 16; Logo reproduced with permission of BMW AG p 16; The Co-operative Bank p 8; Corbis Royalty Free p 32 (Eiffel Tower); C Bartlett p 48; Corbis UK Ltd pp 14 (woman using cell phone/R.W. Jones), 23 (Aristotle Onassis/Bettmann), 24 (waterfall/B Ross), 32 (Julia Roberts/M Gerber, Meryl Streep/M Gerber, Kate Beckinsale/M Gerber), 52 (Sean Connery/Bettmann); Liz Claiborne p 23 (portrait); Digital Vision p 32 (Concorde); Kevin Gaskell p 22; Exxon Mobil p 16; Ikea p 16; The Image Bank pp 4 (businessman/J Homa), 5 (business executives/L Dale Gordon), 12 (smiling female executive/H Sims, female executive/Vital Pictures, young woman/Yang China Tourism Press.Liu), 14 (hotel front desk/B J. Erlanson-Messens), 24 (glass with water/P Cade), 32 (Leaning Tower of Pisa/H Sund, computer virus/L Klove); Mazda p 17; The Nestlé name is reproduced with the kind permission of Société des Produits Nestlé S.A. p 17; Nokia p 16; Novartis p 17; Peter Johnson Entertainments p 35 (Pulsar Laser Activity Centre); Photodisc pp 15, 18 (fuelling an aeroplane), 32 (Champagne, laptop computer, aeroplane); Samsung Electronics p 17; Sony p 16; Stockbyte p 32 (beer, orange juice), p 68 (notepad and pen); Stone pp 4 (young woman/K Weingart), 14 (business executives/I Shaw), 24 (water splashing into hands/Philip & Karen Smith), 32 (palmtop computer/P Dazeley, acrobatic aeroplane/J McBride), 40 (business meeting/D Bosler); Telegraph Colour Library pp 10 (two businesspeople/S W. Jones), 12 (businessman/J Cummins, businessman/Co-Productions, man smiling/F Tousche, businessman/100% Rag Productions), 32 (CN Tower/W Bibikow), 44 (juggling clocks/D Greenwood); United Colours of Benetton p 17; Veronafiere p 28 (Veronafiere); Railman Photo Office (Japanese bullet train) and Photodisc cover

Designed by Shireen Nathoo Design, London